**ADVANCE PRAISE FOR *A WOMAN'S GUIDE
TO SUCCESSFUL NEGOTIATING***

"A useful book for women on the art of
in personal relationships, in every are
—Donna Lagani,
Cosmopolitan **and** *Cosmogirl* **Magazines**

"Lots of practical advice on how to win with a woman's touch.
—Jan Hopkins, Anchor, *CNN Street Sweep*

"The definitive negotiating guide for women. The fact that a
father and daughter could actually get this book to print speaks
volumes about their individual negotiating skills."
—Joan Verplanck, President, **New Jersey
State Chamber of Commerce**

"An invaluable source of wisdom for women, young and old,
who want to take their place in the world."
—Christine Baranski, **Emmy and Tony Award-Winning Actress**

"This is a must-read book for women everywhere, whether a
full-time mom, corporate executive or student. The advice the
authors share to help today's woman succeed in negotiating calls
for a sigh of relief in a competitive, male-dominated world.
Thank you."
—Terrie Williams, **Author of** *The Personal Touch*

"Negotiation is important to every aspect of our lives. . .both
professional and personal. Lee and Jessica Miller have created
a solid reference book that is both helpful and fun to read. I
recommend it enthusiastically."
—Joan Shapiro Green, President, **Financial Women's Association**

OTHER BOOKS BY LEE E. MILLER

Get More Money on Your Next Job: 25 Proven Strategies for Getting More Money, Better Benefits, and Greater Job Security

A Woman's Guide to Successful Negotiating

How to Convince, Collaborate, and Create Your Way to Agreement

by

Lee E. Miller

and

Jessica Miller

McGraw-Hill

New York   Chicago   San Francisco   Lisbon
London   Madrid   Mexico City   Milan   New Delhi
San Juan   Seoul   Singapore   Sydney   Toronto

Library of Congress Cataloging-in-Publication Data

Miller, Lee. E.
    A woman's guide to successful negotiating: how to convince,
    collaborate & create your way to agreement   /   by Lee E. Miller and
    Jessica Miller
       p.   cm.
    Includes index.
    ISBN 0-07-138915-6 (alk. paper)
      1. Negotiation.   2. Women–Psychology.   I. Miller, Jessica.   II. Title

    BF637.N4 M55   2002
    158'.5'082—dc—dc21   2001007961

McGraw-Hill

*À Division of The **McGraw·Hill** Companies*

1 2 3 4 5 6 7 8 9 0   AGM/AGM   0 9 8 7 6 5 4 3 2

ISBN 0-07-138915-6

McGraw-Hill books are available at special quantity discounts to use as premiums and
sales promotions, or for use in corporate training programs. For more information,
please write to the Director of Special Sales, Professional Publishing, McGraw-Hill,
Two Penn Plaza, New York, NY 10121-2298. Or contact your local bookstore.

 This book is printed on recycled, acid-free paper containing a minimum of 50% recycled, de-inked fiber.

We would like to dedicate this book to Samantha, Francia, Joanna, Michelle, Jodie, Rebecca, Lindsey, Brittany, Nicole, Hannah, Taylor, and little Samantha—all the cousins that are young women in our family for whom we hope this book will provide inspiration.

Contents

Foreword

Back in 1987, Missouri Congressman and House Majority Leader Richard A. Gephardt was planning his bid for the White House. I was his deputy press secretary, and a novice to the national political process. But that did not matter at the time. In the arena of national politics, and in business in a sense, all women were novices of a sort. Still, Gephardt understood that to win he needed women. So every week he would gather a broad range of exceptional women from diverse fields for discussions about the issues facing the nation and the world. I was fortunate enough to be a part of those meetings. One thing became very clear to me during those sessions: women of my generation would break barriers as no other generation had before us.

Seven years later, I went to work with Oprah Winfrey. As her top media strategist, I have heard her described as "the most influential person in media," "the most beloved person in America," and "the richest entertainer in America." I tried not to get caught up in the titles. What impressed me the most about her was that she embodied everything that women were striving for during my days on Capitol Hill. She was unlike anyone I had ever encountered. She redefined the path to success by combining business savvy with human compassion. Just as significant, by celebrating her womanhood while dominating a field traditionally controlled by men, she became a role model for millions of women.

I sometimes feel that people make too big a deal about my having worked with rich and famous employers. Although I consider myself fortunate to have had these opportunities, I was raised to believe that I belonged at the table where the stakes were highest. My mother, a southern belle who is warmly direct and can still quiet me with a look, raised me and my five older sisters to embrace our feminine qualities while also learning about the business world from my father, who was the banquet manager of a country club. As women, my mother not only taught us the art of compromising but also to be fearless, focused, and even shrewd, when necessary.

Lee Miller might say that my mother was actually giving us our first lessons in how to negotiate. I met Lee in 1999 after reading his first book, *Get More Money on Your Next Job.* I was so impressed that I picked up the phone and called him. I used the advice in his book to help me successfully negotiate my contract. Since then, I have had the opportunity to spend time with him and have come to regard him as an original thinker and one the best teachers and practitioners in the field of negotiating today. His thoughts on the subject are not only insightful but can be readily put to use in the real world. While I seldom take kindly to men who "meddle in women's business," I believe that negotiating is one of those rare areas in which the male experience wins hands down—at least for now. Having raised two daughters, Lee understands what it takes for women to succeed as negotiators. His oldest daughter and coauthor, Jessica, an investment banker with Deutsche Bank Securities and an outstanding negotiator in her own right, adds her insights to the subject.

Today, women need more than ever to excel in the art of negotiating. If we spent the latter half of the twentieth century getting to the table, the twenty-first century will be all about securing our place at it. To do so, we must not only master all of the essential negotiating skills but also become comfortable with ourselves as negotiators. *A Woman's Guide to Successful Negotiating: How to Convince, Collaborate, and Create Your Way to Agreement* covers everything you need to know to do both. From how to prepare yourself, to what you should know about your adversaries, to when and how to walk away, Lee and Jessica offer practical, easy-to-use advice on negotiating. This book will teach you the skills you need to negotiate in every aspect of your personal and your professional life, including how to buy or sell a house, get a raise, negotiate a divorce settlement, buy a car, and negotiate with your husband, boyfriend, or children.

In *A Woman's Guide to Successful Negotiating,* you will hear from a wide range of women who are themselves skillful negotiators—women like Cathleen Black, president of Hearst Magazines; Lisa Hall, chief operating officer for Oxygen Media; Carolyn Wall, the former publisher of *Newsweek*; Kitty D'Alessio, the first female and the first American president of Chanel; Susanna Hoffs, lead singer of The Bangles, and her mother, Tamar Simon Hoffs, a writer, producer, and director; Lisa Caputo, president of Citigroup's Women & Co. and formerly White House press secretary to Hillary Clinton; Elaine Conway, director of The New York State Commission on Women; Tony and Emmy award–winning actress Christine Baranski; and Katie Blackburn, executive vice president for the NFL Cincinnati Bengals. Their words will inspire lesser-known trailblazers in our classrooms and our boardrooms, in our businesses and in our homes. We've come a long way together, but we still have a long way to go. This book will help to guide us on our journey.

—**Deborah Hayes** is Director, Public Affairs, for the Pew Charitable Trusts and the former Press Secretary for House Majority Leader Richard Gephardt, Director of Media and Corporate Relations for Oprah Winfrey's Harpo Productions, and the Senior Vice President of Corporate Communications for MTV Networks.

Acknowledgments

We would like to give special thanks to our editor, Nancy Hancock, who has supported this project from its inception and whose guidance and insights have been invaluable; and to Deborah Hayes, Director, Public Affairs, the Pew Charitable Trusts; Joseph Cicio, former Chairman, I. Magnin, and Creative Merchandising Consultant; Sara Moe, President, Neighborhood Resource Services; Bonnie St. John, Speaker, Olympic silver medalist and Author of *Getting Ahead at Work Without Leaving Your Family Behind*; Tom Colan, Senior Consultant, KPMG; and Olga Marie Vera, Manager, Moneyline.

We would also like to thank the following women for sharing their wisdom and experience with us: Cathleen Black, President, Hearst Magazines; Lisa Hall, Chief Operating Officer, Oxygen Media; Carol Evans, President and CEO, Working Mother Media; Jan Hopkins, Anchor, CNN Street Sweep; Lisa Caputo, President of Citigroup's Women & Co. and former White House Press Secretary to Hillary Clinton; Katie Ford, Chief Executive Officer, Ford Modeling Agency; Christine Baranski, actress and winner of two Tonys, an Emmy, and two Screen Actors Guild awards; Jeanette Chang, Publishing Director, Hearst Magazine International; Donna Lagani, Publishing Director, Cosmopolitan Group, which publishes *Cosmopolitan* and *CosmoGirl* magazines; Elaine Conway, Director of the New York State Commission on Women; Jerri DeVard, Chief Marketing Officer for Citibank's eConsumer Group; Katie Blackburn, Executive

Vice President, NFL Cincinnati Bengals; Carole Cooper, Owner-Agent, N.S. Bienstock, Inc.; Carol Raphael, President and CEO, Visiting Nurse Service of New York; Gail Evans, former Executive Vice President of CNN, and author of *Play Like a Man, Win Like a Woman*; Susanna Hoffs, lead singer for The Bangles; Tamar Simon Hoffs, producer, writer, and director; Anna Lloyd, President and Executive Director of the Committee of 200; Terrie Williams, President of the Terrie Williams Agency and author of *Personal Touch*; Christina Mohr, Managing Director, Salomon Smith Barney; Judge Kathleen Roberts, Mediator and former United States Magistrate; Susan Medalie, Executive Director, Women's Campaign Fund; Patricia Hambrecht, President, Harry Winston; Carolyn Wall, former Publisher of *Newsweek*; Dee Soder, Ph.D., Founder and Managing Partner, The CEO Perspective Group; Pat Mastandrea, President, The Cheyenne Group; Janice Reals Ellig, Partner, Gould, McCoy and Chaddick and author of *What Every Successful Woman Knows*; Leil Lowndes, author of *How to Make Anyone Fall in Love with You*; G. G. Michelson, former Senior Vice President of External Affairs, R.H. Macy & Co. Inc.; Davia Temin, President, Temin & Co; Cathy Harbin, General Manager, King & Bear and Slammer & Squire golf courses; Robin Tomchin, President, RT Productions; Nancy Settle, General Counsel, L'Oreal Ltd. (UK); Patricia Farrell, Ph.D., professor and clinical psychologist; Terri Santisi, Partner, KPMG, Global Industry Leader Media and Entertainment Group; Randi Kahn, Managing Director, Salomon Smith Barney; Kitty Van Bortel, Owner, Van Bortel Subaru; Kitty D'Alessio, former President, Chanel; Jean Hollands, President, Growth and Leadership Center and author of *Same Game, Different Rules*; Bonnie Stone, President and CEO, Women In Need; Claire Irving and Diana Moneta, Principals, Investigative Consultants LLC; Ellen Sandles, Executive Director, Tri-State Private Investors

Network; Emily Menlo Marks, Executive Director, United Neighborhood Houses of New York; Gina Doynow, Vice President and Manager of College Credit Card Services for Citicorp; Judy Rosemarin, President, Sense-Able Strategies, Inc.; Maxine Hartley, executive coach, Drake Beam Morin; Carolyn Klemm, Owner-Broker, Klemm Real Estate; Lisa Brown, Broker, Stribling Associates; Margery Hadar, Vice President, William B. May Company; Linda Gedney, Broker, Prudential Fox & Roache; Ronna Lichtenberg, President, Clear Peak Communications and author of *It's Not Business It's Personal*; Claire Costello, Vice President, Philanthropic Advisement, Citigroup Private Bank; Joanne Bobes, Manager, Prudential Insurance; Roberta Benjamin, Partner, Benjamin & Benson; Nancy Erika Smith, Partner, Smith & Mullin; Janet Brownlee, Senior Vice President, Human Resources, Donovan Data Systems; Dr. Allison Ashley, Managing Partner, Veracity International; Marcia Lite, Account Executive, Automated Data Processing; and Lynn Fontaine Newsome, Partner, Donahue, Hagan, Klein and Newsome, PC.

Introduction

You Don't Have to Give Up Who You Are to Get What You Want

Jerri DeVard, Chief Marketing Officer for Citibank's eConsumer Group, tells the story about the day her three-year-old son got his first water gun. He ran around shooting everyone he saw. Later that day, a little three-year-old girl friend was dropped off at the house so they could play together. When she saw the water gun, which by now he had grown tired of, lying on the floor, she immediately picked it up and began to water the flowers with it. This story brought home once again for us the fact that men and women see the world very differently, even at a very young age. This is no less true when it comes to how men and women go about trying to get what they want out of life.

How often have you agreed to something, then looked back and wondered, "What was I thinking? How did that ever happen?" You not only didn't get what you wanted—you also agreed to do something you never intended to do. What about that raise you deserve but do not have the nerve to ask your boss for, or the assignment you want that the boss is thinking about giving to someone else? What about your new car, which you like but think you paid too much for? Why is it that you work as hard as your husband but seem to end up doing more than your share around the house? There is an art to getting what you want. It is called negotiating.

I once asked the students in my negotiating class to tell me how they thought their lives would change if they were able to negotiate effectively. One student said, "My car would have cost less. I would make more money. I could get the home I want. And my husband would help more around the house." Another said, "People wouldn't be able to take advantage of me." A third said, "It would give me the confidence to get what I want." Another said, "I could change my community for the better." All these things are possible when you master the art of negotiating. But one student really captured the essence of what negotiating can do for you when she said, "I'd be able to control my own destiny."

Knowing how to negotiate will empower you. You will decide what to agree to and what you are not willing to accept. You will be able to shape situations to ensure that your interests are protected. Although you may not always get everything you want, you will get more than you ever imagined you could. More often than not, you will not only get what you want, but also you will help others accomplish their objectives at the same time. In the final chapter of this book, we will show you how to take what you have learned from this book and put it into practice. You will progress through the three stages of change needed to become a better negotiator—illumination, progression, and transformation. By following the program we outline, you will learn how to negotiate and will develop the skills and attitudes of an effective negotiator. Once you have reached the third stage, negotiating will become a natural part of who you are.

If you are like most women, you don't feel completely comfortable negotiating. It is not something you were taught to do when you were growing up. In fact, young girls are often taught, subtly and not so subtly, to defer or manipulate rather than negotiate, especially in their dealings with men. They are expected to use their "feminine wiles" to get what they want because it has not been considered "ladylike" to negotiate with men.

As Cathleen Black, President of Hearst Magazines, which publishes *Marie Claire, Cosmopolitan, "O," Redbook,* and *Harper's Bazaar,* notes, "Some women are uncomfortable with the word *negotiating.* They consider it a tough, hard, male word." Yet you are negotiating all day, every day, even though you may not think of it that way. You negotiate with your husband about who will make breakfast for the kids, about what kind of car to purchase, and about whether to buy a new refrigerator or to just fix the old one. You negotiate with your boyfriend about what movie to see and whether or not to have a big wedding. You negotiate with your boss about getting a raise, about the time off you need, or about an assignment you want. You negotiate with customers and vendors about prices and delivery schedules. You negotiate with friends about where to go on vacation or where to go for dinner. You negotiate with your children about curfews, allowances, and chores. And you negotiate when you buy a car, buy or sell a house, or get a divorce.

Suppose you are at a restaurant with a friend and she asks, "Would you like to share a piece of apple pie for dessert?" When you reply, "I really feel like having chocolate cake," you are negotiating. Whenever two people don't agree, they negotiate. They may not sit around a bargaining table or make proposals and counterproposals, but the only way two people can reach workable solutions is by negotiating. As Emily Menlo Marks, Executive Director of United Neighborhood Houses of New York, puts it: "All life is a negotiation. It's not a question of liking or not liking to negotiate. It's a matter of doing it."

If you think of children dividing up a loaf of bread as negotiating, then it loses some of its negative connotations. Dividing up the bread does not mean that one person gets the whole loaf and the others get only crumbs. Rather, they can divide it up fairly, in a way that fosters their continuing friendship. If one has bread, another has peanut butter, and a third has jelly, the benefits of negotiating are obvious. Once you understand that negotiating is really about obtaining someone else's help to get what you want, you readily recognize that arguing, screaming, and haggling are rarely effective. Common sense tells you that those tactics will not work with people you have, or want to establish, a relationship with. Those are the very people with whom you have the most important negotiations. They are your bosses, coworkers, husbands, boyfriends, family members, friends, vendors, customers, and prospective customers.

Nancy Settle, General Counsel for L'Oreal Ltd., (U.K.), the multinational cosmetic company whose brands include Maybelline, Lancome, and Redken, negotiates for a living and she is very good at it. Yet when asked if she likes to negotiate, she responded, "No, it's too contentious." She is not the only woman we interviewed who felt that way. If an accomplished negotiator feels like that, we have little doubt you probably share that feeling. But it doesn't have to be that way. Most of the women we interviewed admitted that they actually enjoy negotiating—now that they are comfortable with the process.

Men and women view negotiations differently. As Gail Evans, a former Executive Vice President at CNN and author of *Play*

Like a Man, Win Like a Woman, told us, "Women are different. We were brought up differently; we think differently." To understand how those differences affect the way women negotiate, you need to recognize that negotiations involve not only outcomes but relationships as well.

All negotiations can be seen as falling somewhere on a continuum in terms of the importance we place on each of these two dimensions: the outcome and the relationship. On one end of the continuum are negotiations in which you care a lot about the outcome and almost nothing about the relationship, such as when you negotiate with a used car salesman. You are dealing with a stranger whom you don't trust and will probably never see again; all you really care about are features and price. On the other end of the spectrum are negotiations with a boss or potential business partners with whom you will continue to work in the future. In these situations, any one deal is much less important than the working relationship as a whole. Similarly, many negotiations with family and friends fall on the relationship end of the continuum. However, always giving in, even when something is important to you, can create problems in a relationship.

Although the relationship dimension exists to some degree in most negotiations, women tend to place greater importance on the relationship in almost every type of negotiation. Men tend to remain focused on outcomes while making an effort to avoid damaging relationships they care about. For men, relationships are a means to the end. For women, relationships are an end in and of themselves, wholly separate from any tangible benefits they can derive from them. The intrinsic value women place on relationships affects how they view negotiations. As a result, women sometimes allow relationships to get in the way of achieving their desired outcomes.

Women can, however, use their relationship skills to help them negotiate better. In writing this book, we have developed a way of thinking about negotiations that works for both men and women but is particularly powerful for women. Our approach recognizes the importance that women place on relationships and treats that as a strength, not a weakness.

Our negotiating model consists of three basic approaches from which you can choose at different times during negotiation: convince, collaborate, and create.

Convince refers to changing the way the person you are dealing with sees things. It draws from the study of rhetoric (persuasion), body language, and traditional distributive negotiating tactics. You accomplish what you want by convincing others that it is in their interest to do what you are proposing or that what you are suggesting supports values that are important to them. In Chapter 3, we provide you with tools such as active listening, purposeful questioning, using concessions, and anchoring that will enable you to persuade someone to your point of view.

Collaborate refers to both sides changing the negotiating focus to one of problem solving. The goal is to find ways to satisfy everyone's interests. Collaborate incorporates and expands upon the "win-win" negotiating model. You achieve your objectives by working with someone to come up with a solution that accommodates everyone's interests. In Chapter 4, you learn how to use tools such as "coupling interests," "trading," and "expanding the pie" to reach mutually satisfactory agreements.

Create refers to changing the way you negotiate by taking a fresh look at how you have done things in the past and coming up with more effective ways to achieve your objectives. Create helps you to find ways to negotiate that better fit your needs or your negotiating style. As discussed in Chapter 5, sometimes the best way to get what you want is to create a whole new way of resolving the issue—a different negotiating paradigm. In any particular negotiation, you may emphasize one of these three as your primary approach. However, you can use all three, in varying degrees, in almost every negotiating situation.

Judge Kathy Roberts, a professional mediator and former United States Magistrate, summarizes our basic philosophy when she says:

> Women often underestimate the value of having a full repertoire of negotiating skills. A lot of women are more open to the win-win, problem-solving approach and really don't learn the skills you need where the situation is fundamentally distributive and you are dividing up the pie. Women need to learn how to use all those skills together. They need to be more sophisticated in how they approach negotiating.

The best negotiators convince and collaborate simultaneously. Create can also be added to the mix in most negotiations. We will teach you to recognize when conditions are right to emphasize a collaborative approach and when your primary approach should be to convince or create. As you become a more skilled negotiator, you will learn how and when to shift approaches within any given situation.

> I wanted to coauthor this book with my dad because of how my ability to negotiate has helped me throughout my life. As I look back on my early childhood, it is obvious that the lessons my dad wants to impart to our readers are the same ones I learned from him at a very early age. When I was growing up, most of my negotiations involved relationships and situations you would not ordinarily think of as negotiations. Today I constantly negotiate in business as well as in my personal life. This book provides an opportunity to share the lessons I learned from my dad.

Jessica's qualifications to coauthor this book are obvious. She is a magna cum laude finance major from Virginia Tech and she is an investment banker with Deutsche Bank Securities. She has won all sorts of awards for her leadership and, as an exceptional negotiator, she can provide unique insights into what it takes for a woman to negotiate successfully.

You may be asking yourself what qualifies me to write this book. I could talk about my training at Harvard Law School, my years practicing law as a partner in one of the preeminent national employment law firms where I negotiated labor contracts and employment agreements, my experience as Vice President of Labor Relations at Macy's or as head of human resources at Barneys New York, USA Networks, and *TV Guide* Magazine, my experience teaching negotiating to both men and women in the MBA program at Seton Hall University, or the classes on negotiating I teach to women. I could also point to the interviews we conducted with successful women across a wide range of fields.

However, what truly qualifies me to write this book is that I am the father of two exceptional daughters. I wanted to equip them to be successful in their personal and professional lives, and to do that, one of the things I taught them was how to negotiate. That is also why I wanted to write this book with Jessica.

No woman to whom we have spoken about this project has been anything but enthusiastic. We became convinced that there was a critical need for this book when the 25-year-old female public relations executive assigned to evaluate the idea told our editor, "If we don't publish this, I want to know who the publisher is because this is a book I have to read." Now that the book is finished, we are just as convinced of the need for it as we were when we started.

1

The Three Keys to Success:

Be Confident, Be Prepared, and Be Willing to Walk Away

In writing this book we interviewed women from all walks of life—corporate executives, lawyers, publishers, politicians, entre-preneurs, writers, musicians, actresses, agents, philanthropists, athletes—all very successful. Most have strong collaborative skills, many are extremely persuasive, and some excel at taking the negotiating situation they find and creating a different one that better suits their needs. Interestingly, almost universally they listed three qualities that are critical to success as negotiators: confidence, preparation, and a willingness to walk away. These three qualities do not fall neatly within one of the convince, collaborate, or create categories, but rather are central to all three approaches. They are attitudes you bring to negotiations. They are the underpinnings that enable someone to effectively use each of the three approaches. So we have devoted a separate section to them.

BE CONFIDENT: WHY MEN DON'T ASK FOR DIRECTIONS

Class is an aura of confidence that is being sure without being cocky. Class has nothing to do with money....It is self-discipline and self-knowledge. It's the sure-footedness that comes with having proved you can meet life.
—ANN LANDERS

Susanna Hoffs had just put together The Bangles, which would become the dominant all-female rock band of the 1980s, garner four platinum albums and many hit singles, and see "Walk Like an Egyptian" and "Eternal Flame" make it to the top of the charts. She was performing with the band at a local club. Miles Copeland, the manager who had engineered the earlier success of the Go-Gos, approached them after the show to talk about representing them. Rather than acting as if she should be grateful for his interest, Susanna "took the position that he should want to work with us because we were going places." It helped, of course, that at the time she had no idea who Miles Copeland was, and therefore didn't know she should be nervous. Because of the confidence with which Susanna and the other Bangles approached those negotiations, they were able to work out a favorable deal to have Miles manage the group.

Confidence is the secret weapon in negotiating. Almost every woman we interviewed pointed to it as the key to their success as a negotiator. To gain agreement from others, you need to persuade them that what you are proposing is based on an accurate understanding of the facts, is fair, and is mutually beneficial.

Studies have shown that whether someone believes what you say depends more on how you say it than on what you actually say. Put another way, to be truly persuasive, whatever you say, you must say with confidence.

You can take several steps to build your confidence. Reading this book is a good start. Understanding the negotiating process will add to your self-confidence. Often you will instinctively do the right thing, and all you need is confirmation of that. One of the nicest things anyone said about my first book, *Get More Money on Your Next Job,* which dealt with negotiating in the employment context, came from a young woman who told me that reading it gave her the confidence to ask a prospective employer to pay for her MBA. As she said, it "affirmed that what I was doing was okay."

Practice

Take the skills you learn from this book and put them to use on a daily basis. Practice the active listening and purposeful questioning skills we discuss in Chapter 3 until you master them. You don't have to wait for opportunities to negotiate to do this. Try using them at the dinner table with your husband and children. When others ask you for something, or you hear them ask someone else for something, try to use the collaborative skill of determining the underlying interests they are trying to satisfy. In the last chapter of the book, we set out a program for taking the lessons you'll learn here and using them to transform yourself into an effective negotiator. A critical element of that program is to develop the necessary skills and attitudes through practice.

Like driving a car, negotiating is a skill that you must learn. After you finish reading the driver's manual and get your learner's permit, you do not just get into the car for the first time and know how to drive. You take a driver's education class in school, you take driving lessons, or a parent or a friend teaches you. While taking lessons, you also practice driving. You practice turning. You practice merging into traffic. You practice parallel parking, and then you practice parallel parking some more. Similarly, to master negotiating you must not only learn how to do it; you must also practice it. The more you practice, the more comfortable you will become. Remember how nervous you were the first time you drove on a highway? By now, you no longer give it a second thought. Like driving, once you have done it enough, negotiating becomes second nature.

Find Out About the People on the Other Side

Another way to boost your confidence is to learn as much as you can about the people you are negotiating with. As Judge Kathy Roberts, a professional mediator and former U.S. Magistrate, said:

> It is amazing that people don't do research about their adversaries. This is particularly important for women because if you find out about your opponent you will be more confident. You will know what to expect. You can anticipate things. If you know someone is known for threatening to walk out at some point or for taunting women, you will not have the same reaction because you know it's coming. You will have thought out how you will respond when it happens.

The best way to find out about those with whom you are negotiating is to ask people who know them and who have negotiated with them before. The more you know about what to expect, the more confident you will be.

Confidence Equals Success

The more confidence you exude, the better you will negotiate. Conversely, insecurity reduces effectiveness, and a lack of success will further hurt your confidence. Because women typically do not learn to negotiate when they are growing up, as adults they are uncomfortable with their ability to do so. This lack of confidence frequently translates into poor results. So, they come to believe they are bad negotiators, when in fact they simply lack experience. Like any other skill, negotiating can be learned. And you should consider any negotiation successful if you learn something from it. Moreover, a negotiation does not necessarily end if you don't immediately reach an agreement. Sometimes a negotiation just changes venues. You will generally have other opportunities to get what you want by going back and trying again—with the same party at a later date, with someone else, or in some other way. The lessons you learn from one negotiation will help you in your next negotiation and every one thereafter.

Act Confident

Until you have gained sufficient confidence by mastering negotiating skills, simply act as if you know what you are doing: "Fake it until you make it." That is what men do. Men are every bit as uncomfortable as women when it comes to doing things that are new to them. The difference is that men are raised not to show their fear. While growing up, they do not share their insecurities with their friends. Instead, they learn to put on a show of bravado. If someone pushes them, they push back—no matter how big the pusher or how scared they are. Boys seldom display fear in front of their male friends or, heaven forbid, a girlfriend. In fact, the more nervous men are, the more confident they try to act. Have you ever noticed how many men spend an entire first date talking about how terrific they are (even though this often results in it being their last date)? This is not just ego. It is nervousness, masked by bravado.

This is why men don't ask for directions. They do not want to display weakness. They would rather drive around aimlessly for hours. When you are lost, not asking for directions is silly. When you are negotiating, acting confident even when you are not, works. So, regardless of how you actually feel, act as if you are in control of the situation.

Exhibit confidence through the words you use, by the way you speak, and with your demeanor. Use positive body language to signal confidence. Move forward to your audience. Uncross your arms. Use open-hand, palms-up gestures. Unbutton your jacket. Look the other person in the eye. Show that you are in control.

TIPS FOR PROJECTING CONFIDENCE

Prepare.

Psyche yourself up.

Take a deep breath, exhale, and relax.

Smile.

Stand or sit up straight.

Don't fidget.

Speak slowly.

Be firm.

Moderate your tone.

Project your voice.

Patricia Farrell, Ph.D., professor of clinical psychology at Walden University, advises: psych yourself up before you begin. She calls this "self-talk." Convince yourself that your position is right and that you deserve to get what you are seeking. If you believe it, so will the people you are negotiating with. Once you begin negotiating, smile, look people in the eye, speak slowly, don't fidget, moderate your tone, and project your voice.

Demonstrate that you are capable of being firm. It is okay to speak softly as long as you speak with conviction. We are referring to a quiet confidence, not arrogance or bravado. When you negotiate, you don't have to know every detail. In fact, sometimes admitting that you do not know or don't remember something actually enhances your credibility. However, admitting to not knowing a detail is not the same as failing to display confidence in the positions you are advocating. Avoid confusing them.

Carol Raphael, President and CEO of The Visiting Nurses Service of New York, was advised by a top labor negotiator the first time she had to negotiate a labor agreement to "act decisively and exude confidence, even if you're quaking inside." She has taken that advice, and not only with regard to union negotiations. No matter what she is feeling, she acts decisively: "Sometimes I will step out of the room and may feel queasy and uncomfortable, but no one will ever know it because when I walk back in the room I am unflappable." Remember the tagline from the old Secret deodorant commercials, "Never let them see you sweat"? That is good advice when you negotiate. If you are in doubt about what to do, find an excuse to take a break and seek advice.

A corollary to being confident is not to be apologetic about the positions you are taking, particularly if you are negotiating with men. Women often start off their statements with phrases such as "You may have already considered this, but..." or "I could be wrong, but..." Men view such statements as signs of weakness and lack of conviction. Regardless of what you say after that, men will assume that you are willing to back off from your position. Instead, show that you want to collaborate. Be magnanimous. Say things like, "That's a good point" or "I've thought about what you said and..." Such statements do not show a lack of confidence, but rather that you are confident enough in your position to modify it to accommodate their concerns. Ultimately, as one senior executive we interviewed put it: "When you're dealing with men, never apologize unless you step on their foot."

BE PREPARED, OR BE PREPARED TO FAIL

I'm a great believer in luck, and I find the harder I work the more I have of it.
—Thomas Jefferson

Negotiations are won or lost before you ever utter a word to the other party. Proper preparation is critical to achieving a successful outcome. Skilled negotiators understand the importance of preparation. Most of the women we interviewed even used the same phrase: "Do your homework." Preparation may involve months of research, or as little as a few minutes that you set aside to think about things before you begin. Many of the negotiations you encounter on a daily basis will allow you almost no time to prepare. Although each situation is different, here are some basic steps you should take before every negotiation.

Gather the Necessary Information

We cannot overemphasize the importance of understanding the facts, the players, and the rules of the game. Before you begin to negotiate, gain a thorough mastery of the facts. Figure out which questions you want to ask, both to gain information and to make a point. Anticipate what questions the other side will ask, and determine how you plan to respond to them.

Gather information about both the facts and the people with whom you'll be dealing. Are they honest? Can you trust them? Will they try to intimidate you? Do you know anyone in common? What is their negotiating style?

You should also try to find out how the other side expects the negotiations to proceed. Who do they expect will make the initial offer, how long do they think the process should take, and what do they define as proper etiquette. In other words, what are the rules of the game? Once you understand that, you can choose an appropriate strategy for playing the game—or whether this is even a game you want to play.

Once you have gathered the basic facts, done your analysis, and figured out what you want, you are ready to get started. You can never know everything, but you can continue gathering information and making adjustments as you go along. Negotiating is an adaptive process. Today's world moves at "Internet speed." We are a society operating in real time, so making decisions or taking actions based on incomplete information is unavoidable. Prepare as much as you reasonably can, then move forward with confidence, knowing that you are probably better prepared than the person with whom you are dealing, particularly if you are negotiating with a man.

Decide on Your Goals and Objectives

In any negotiation you must determine what you really want. As Yogi Berra once said, "If you don't know where you're going, any road will get you there." Make a list of the things you would like to get, and prioritize which are most important. When you are developing your list, think about your underlying interests, not just what you want. Interests are *why* we want the things that we want. For example, you may want to purchase the empty lot next to your house to assure that your view of the lake remains unobstructed. Buying the property is what you want, but your reason is to prevent anything from being built that would impair your view. Focusing on your real interests as well as your neighbors' may make a difference if they don't want to sell. Once you focus on your real interest, you will see that there are other ways to satisfy it than by purchasing the property. For example, you could get your neighbors to agree not to build anything that would obstruct your view, in return for allowing them to share your driveway from the main road when they begin construction.

Determine the Other Person's Interests

Begin by finding out everything you can about the people with whom you are negotiating. What are their interests? What do they want? Why do they want it? What do they really need? To do that, you may need to determine who besides the negotiator has a say in the outcome. When you are selling your house, for example, the real estate broker may be talking to the husband, but his wife may be calling the shots. If you want to close the deal, you must find out what she cares about. In that example, you could probably find out who is making the decisions and what is important to them by asking the real estate broker. Bonnie Stone, President and Chief Executive Officer of Women In Need, a nonprofit organization that runs homeless shelters, said it well:

> Do your homework, and do the other person's homework. You need to know exactly what their needs are. The more you know, the easier it will be to craft a deal. To be successful, you have to know what the other person needs and wants.

How do you do that? Put yourself in their shoes. Think about what you would want if you were they. If the other party is your husband, or someone you know well, you will probably have an accurate sense of how they think. If you don't know the other parties, talk to people who do. Avoid the "I" perspective, that is, looking at issues from your viewpoint rather than looking at them from the other person's perspective.

Talking to people who know the industry and understand the issues can give you insight into how the other side looks at things. Sometimes it helps to have an informal meeting before you actually start negotiating. This also gives you a chance to discuss how the negotiations will proceed, to figure out what the issues are, or simply to get to know each other a little better. Preliminary meetings are a perfect opportunity to find out what the other side wants and needs. They will tell you. All you have to do is ask and then listen.

Determine the Range of Possible Agreement

Let's say you are talking with a prospective home buyer and the lowest price you would be willing to accept is $240,000. Let's assume that the most the prospective buyer is willing to pay (something you won't know with certainty) is $250,000. The range of possible settlement lies between $240,000 and $250,000. If you could figure out that $250,000 was the buyer's maximum, you would hold out until you got $250,000 or an amount close to that. The more accurate you are in determining the other side's range, the better you will be able to negotiate. One way to estimate ranges is by looking at the information available to the other side. In this case, you would probably determine the market value for this type of home by looking at what similar homes in the neighborhood have sold for recently.

Keep in mind that most negotiations involve more than one issue. This allows for trade-offs between different issues, thereby creating opportunities to expand the range of possible agreement on any single issue. For example, in the employment context you may be able to negotiate a greater total compensation package if you are willing to accept a lower base salary in return for a larger potential bonus. Moreover, people are often willing to give more than they initially had intended either because you persuade them they should or simply because the negotiation has proceeded to the point that they have become psychologically invested in ensuring its success.

Identify All the Possible Outcomes

Try to develop an exhaustive list of options, and avoid making judgments until you have completed the list. Only after you have developed a comprehensive list should you try to determine which outcomes would be best for you. For example, if you are negotiating with an employer, you might consider a low salary with high bonus potential, a high salary with low bonus opportunity, more time off in return for a lower total compensation package whether high salary/low bonus or low salary/high bonus, etc. Simply having a complete list will help you to be creative once negotiations begin and you start hearing from the other side.

Determine Your BATNA

As part of your preparation, you must also identify your options in the event that you cannot reach an agreement. From among those, determine your BATNA. This term, coined by Roger Fisher and William Ury in their seminal work on negotiating, *Getting to Yes,* stands for the "best alternative to a negotiated agreement." Put simply, it is what happens if you can't agree. As the term "best" implies, you can have only one BATNA. Your BATNA determines the point at which accepting an offer doesn't make sense because you have a better option available. Knowing your BATNA enables you to negotiate better because you know what to expect if you cannot reach agreement. For example, if you have offered $200,000 to buy a house and the seller refuses to accept, if your BATNA is a house down the street that you like almost as much and can purchase for

$195,000, you are not likely to increase your offer. As we will discuss later, your BATNA determines the point at which you will walk away.

Decide on an Approach

Are you going to try to convince, collaborate, create, or use some combination of all three to achieve your goals? Look at yourself. Consider how you negotiate, your strengths and weaknesses. Then consider those of the other party. Ask yourself how the negotiations would normally proceed. Then decide if you want to use a create approach to change the negotiating paradigm. Determine who should make the first offer. (See discussion of Anchoring at pp. 75–81.) Then choose your strategy for handling the negotiations. After you do that, develop an initial offer consistent with your approach.

Prepare Appropriately

Not every negotiation calls for hours or weeks of preparation. Your daily interactions, such as deciding what movie you and your friends will attend, do not require much preparation. But knowing where and when the movies are playing and having read the reviews will certainly give you a leg up in influencing the decision. Moreover, sometimes you will encounter situations in which you have no time to prepare. Even if you just have a few minutes, though, spend them thinking about what you want to do. Jot down a few thoughts. List what you want to get out of the negotiation. Determine your bottom line—the least you would be willing to accept. Figure out what the other side wants to get out of the negotiations and how you can help satisfy those interests. Come up with a few talking points as to why the other party should want to do what you are proposing. Then decide on your opening offer, or your response if the other side has already made or will make the first offer.

FIVE-MINUTE NEGOTIATING PREP

List your goals.

Determine your bottom line.

Identify the other side's interest.

Outline your opening offer.

List three ways your proposal satisfies the other party's interests.

Being well prepared gives you not only an advantage in the negotiations but also confidence. The better prepared you are, the more confident you will be. That confidence will enable you to be a better negotiator.

BE WILLING TO WALK AWAY: NO DEAL IS BETTER THAN A BAD DEAL

True luck consists not in holding the best of the cards at the table; luckiest is he who knows just when to rise and go home.
—JOHN HAY

If you *must* make this deal, if you *must* have this apartment, or if you simply *must* go to a certain restaurant, you won't negotiate well. You will pay too much, give too much, or just plain get "walked over." Women want to be liked, and they care about what others think of them. They tend to blame themselves when they cannot reach agreement. As a result, they find it difficult to walk away. Men, on the other hand, usually blame the other person when they can't reach an agreement, so they have less difficulty walking away from deals not to their liking. Whether you are a man or a woman, though, to be a good negotiator you must be willing to walk away. Even if you have a great poker face, somehow the other side will sense your need to do the deal. Whether you are negotiating with an investment banker, your boss, or your boyfriend, they will take advantage of the fact that you are not psychologically prepared to walk away. Even though you may not think so at the time, there is always another deal, another job, or another boyfriend. There will always be other opportunities.

Christine Baranski, costar of the long-running television series *Cybil,* is a gifted actress who has won two Tony Awards, an Emmy, and two Screen Actors Guild Awards for her work in film, theater, and television. Yet she believes that early in her career she gave up too much when she negotiated because she lacked confidence and cared too much about what other people thought about her. Over time she has come to recognize not only the need to make clear from the start what is important to her but also the power of being willing to walk away. When she was negotiating to produce and star in the television series *Welcome to New York,* having time with her children was a priority and she wanted the network to accommodate her. To do so, the show had to be shot on the East Coast and the shooting schedule had to allow her time with her children, including a two-week Christmas break. She didn't scream or shout or carry on to get what she wanted. She just made it clear, through her agent, that she needed those accommodations or she would not do the show. The most important thing was that she meant it. Because she was willing to give up the deal, she got what she asked for.

You don't have to be a star to get what you want. You do need to understand the value of what you bring to the table and refuse to accept less. Although it is easier to determine the value of a car you are selling than your own worth, you determine value the same way. Consider the market and your other options. As discuss in Chapter 2, many women undervalue their own worth, so it's good practice to review your analysis with someone else.

Once you determine your bottom line, though, there's no greater power than being willing to walk away.

A good negotiator does everything reasonably possible to arrive at an agreement, starting with proper preparation. If you try to understand what the other side needs, and are creative in your approach, you can usually reach an agreement. Because women tend to be more patient and often are willing to work at it longer, they can sometimes find a way to reach an agreement when a man might not. But if you reach a point when what the other side is insisting on just doesn't make sense for you, you must be willing to walk away. Sometimes, not always, that will cause the other side to reconsider its position. However, no deal is almost always better than a bad deal.

As discussed previously, your preparation should include determining your BATNA—the best option available to you if you do not reach agreement. This is critical not only to being able to walk away but also to knowing when to do so. Knowing that you have an alternative that is at least as good as what you are being offered makes it easier to walk away. Whether you are buying a car, seeking a raise, or determining where to go on vacation with your friends, determining your BATNA will greatly enhance your ability to bargain effectively.

Leil Lowndes, the author of *How to Make Anyone Fall in Love With You,* understands the importance of being willing to walk away. She described a situation earlier in her career when she was booking entertainment for cruise lines. She was trying to convince the entertainment director for American Hawaiian Cruise Lines to book musicals. His reaction to her presentation indicated to her that he was either not interested or was pretending not to be to strengthen his bargaining position. Either way, she figured she might as well leave. So she said, "Well, I know you think this isn't for you, so I might as well go." With that, she got up from her chair and started to leave. He obviously hadn't expected that reaction and called after her, "Now wait a minute." So she sat back down and eventually he agreed to book *South Pacific* and *My Fair Lady* for his upcoming cruises.

Whether you are negotiating with a car dealer, your husband, or your boss, confidence, preparation, and a willingness to walk away will help you get what you want. Remember, sometimes the best result is to agree to disagree. In many cases, no agreement is better than an agreement that fails to satisfy your needs.

2

An error doesn't become a mistake until you refuse to correct it.

—ORLANDO A. BATTISTA

The 10 Most Common Mistakes Women Make and How to Avoid Them

Several common themes ran through the interviews for this book regardless of the age or experience of the women being interviewed. For one thing, it was surprising how many of them had made similar mistakes at some point during their careers. Based on those interviews and Jessica's own experiences, as well as my observations working with women, we have identified 10 common mistakes that women make. Fortunately, once you recognize that you are making them, these mistakes are remarkably easy to avoid.

BE YOURSELF: BUT BE THE BEST SELF YOU CAN BE

Seek out that particular mental attribute which makes you feel most deeply and vitally alive, along with which comes the inner voice which says, "This is the real me," and when you have found that attitude, follow it.
—WILLIAM JAMES

Women often think that good negotiators act tough, scream, know all the tricks, and outsmart their opponents. So if they are seeking to be successful negotiators, that is who they try to become. It usually doesn't work. Why not? In the first place, that type of negotiating doesn't even work for most men, despite the fact that many of them adopt that style. Women are generally more successful when they negotiate if they don't try to "negotiate like a man." Most women prefer a "Relational Negotiating Style" and are uncomfortable with a "Competitive Negotiating Style" (see box at p. 130). To be successful, choose a negotiating style that makes you feel comfortable and reflects who you are. If you aren't authentic, people will see right through it, and you will lose all credibility.

This point was driven home to me in one of my negotiating classes. One of my students, a genuinely nice guy—about 5'7" tall, a little overweight, balding, and always with a smile—did not do well in the early negotiating exercises, so he decided to try a different approach. When he got to a critical juncture during the next exercise, he stood up and started yelling and pounding on the table. Everyone, including his own teammates, had the same reaction: They all burst into laughter. His behavior just wasn't "him," and it certainly wasn't effective.

><+>-O-<+><

Negotiate in a way that works for you. In my business and in my personal life, when I want something I try to figure out a way to get it while still being fair to all parties involved. I trust my instincts and try to be myself. I try to incorporate my own personality into every negotiating situation. I am firm, but I try to be enthusiastic and friendly. For instance, getting angry has never worked well for me, but using my youth to my advantage seems to work with most people I meet for the first time, especially if they are older.

▷—◇——O—◈—◁

Terri Santisi, who heads KPMG's Media and Entertainment Group, describes the way she negotiates as "professional." She does not show her emotions, she stays focused on the issues, and she seeks to maintain a professional demeanor at all times. She is comfortable with that, and it works for her. She says coaches have told her she should try being "more vulnerable." She has tried, but it doesn't work. It is just not her.

People see right through you if you try to be something you're not. If you're soft-spoken, you can be a soft-spoken negotiator and still take strong positions. You can disagree politely. You can provide your reasons for seeing things differently. You can offer alternatives. Although you can be flexible in how you satisfy those interests, you must be able to disagree rather than just giving in to something contrary to your interests. This is what we call being "quietly firm"—which is very powerful because when you do raise your voice, even just a little, people will notice. They will know that you are serious.

When I was graduating from law school and interviewing for jobs, the conventional wisdom was that, when they interviewed, women should wear skirts with matching jackets, typically navy blue, white blouses, and little floppy bow ties. This outfit resembled the suits men wore but failed to project the power image of the three-piece suit we favored at the time. The message being given to women was that they needed to be like men if they wanted to succeed. Author and former CNN executive, Gail Evans, described this as "looking like a junior man." For most women, this attire didn't produce the desired effect because it wasn't authentic. In fact, it made them look silly. Today, women realize that they don't have to dress like a man to be successful in business and have jettisoned the "junior man" uniform in favor of dresses, tailored suits, pants or whatever outfits suit their personality and the occasion.

> As a young investment banker, I usually wear gray or black pantsuits when I visit clients and casual pants and blouses to the office. This wardrobe makes the right impression and looks good on me. When I look good, I feel confident. Every industry has different norms for what to wear. To get an idea of how you should dress, watch what the most successful women at your company wear at different times. Then choose the types of clothes that look good on you and that you are comfortable wearing.

Although ultimatums, threats, screaming, stonewalling, taking extreme positions, and other hardball tactics do not work for most women, that does not mean that women cannot be tough negotiators. In fact, you can be even tougher than a man and get away with it, if you do it right. Acting the part of the "tough negotiator" is different from delivering a tough message. You can deliver that message firmly but in a way that you feel comfortable with, or you can find other ways to have it delivered, such as having someone else deliver it for you. What you cannot do is be something you're not. Worse, negotiating like a man can conjure up the negative stereotype that for lack of a better word we will refer to as the "bitch" stereotype.

The reality is, women are held to a different standard than men. Susan Medalie, currently Executive Director of the Women's Campaign Fund, first witnessed this double standard when she was just starting out in government. She was working for an incredibly talented and able woman who was Secretary of the U.S. Department of Health and Human Services. Whenever this woman expressed anger at her staff, even though it was deserved, some of the men were quick to label her a "bitch" behind her back. On the other hand, when her male predecessor had engaged in similar behavior, it was excused because he was considered a "go-getter."

This stereotype is doubly pernicious. When a woman comes on too strong, men see it as giving them license to disregard not only the woman's position but to disregard her as well. Moreover, some women, to avoid being labeled a "bitch," are cowed into giving up too easily on getting what they want when in fact they could get it if they merely held firm rather than giving in. The problem is usually not with the message but how it is delivered. It is important to ask for what you want, but how you ask matters. For example, men react negatively when a woman presents them with an ultimatum. Telling them quietly and firmly, and as often as necessary, that you really need something accomplishes the same objective without causing a negative reaction. As Jan Hopkins, the anchor for CNN's *Street Sweep* says:

> You have to be careful about "demands." You can't come across as a "bitch." It turns a lot of people off in a negotiating situation. Sometimes you get more by being charming.

Although being loud, sarcastic, intimidating, or even just unnecessarily tough may not actually serve men well, other men will often overlook, accept, or even forgive their behavior. Not so for women. Women who engage in this type of behavior quickly get labeled "bitch," although rarely to their face, by the men with whom they are negotiating. They also frequently find themselves marginalized or taken out of a negotiation altogether because men don't want to work with them. And because women often work for men, the men they are negotiating with can go directly to the boss. This can hurt not only your ability to negotiate effectively but also damage your career. By using the principles set forth in this book, you can be firm and not give in, without the threat of being labeled a "bitch."

Jean Hollands, CEO and President of The Growth and Leadership Center and the author of *Same Game, Different*

Rules: How to Get Ahead Without Being a Bully Broad, Ice Queen or "Ms. Understood," works with women who are about to derail their careers because their companies consider them too aggressive. Some women come to her believing they can get what they want if they "just bark loud enough, because they have seen it work for men." But it doesn't work for them. She advises women to soften their approach by showing vulnerability, which she calls the "flip side of anger." This allows them to press the logic of their position without risking being perceived as overly aggressive or difficult. She says that women can be effective if they talk about their feelings, because "they are being authentic." For example, rather than saying, "I deserved to go to the conference, but you stupidly chose Charlie instead," a woman could say, "I was really hurt that you chose Charlie to go to the conference instead of me. I wanted to go. It would have helped me with the project I am working on for the company."

Women who are successful with an aggressive, "competitive style" succeed because it is natural for them. They are naturally competitive, they like to win, and they have learned how to do it with grace and style. Humor can soften the impact of a "competitive style" and allow a woman to employ it effectively. As Carolyn Wall, former Publisher of *Newsweek,* puts it, "They can do it because they do it with charm. Charm is their secret weapon." Janice Reals Ellig, a partner in the executive search firm of Gould, McCoy and Chaddick and the author of *What Every Successful Woman Knows,* suggests that one way for a woman to avoid being seen as too aggressive is "not to keep pushing" if you encounter strong resistance. Instead she suggests "letting it go for a while and then coming back to it." CNN anchor Jan Hopkins, likens this to her interviewing approach: "You come back to the same issue several different times and in several different ways."

Always negotiate in a way that is consistent with who you are. That doesn't mean that you cannot change to make yourself a better negotiator or adjust your approach when you are negotiating with someone who has a different style. Learn to recognize your strengths and weaknesses. Watch how different types of people react to you. Ask people who have seen you negotiate how they see your strengths and weaknesses. This self-awareness will help you play to your strengths and compensate for your weaknesses. It will also enable you to recognize when you lack the skills, style, or patience needed in a particular situation so you can bring in someone else to handle all or part of the negotiating.

IT DOESN'T HURT TO ASK: ALMOST EVERYTHING IS NEGOTIABLE

You may be disappointed if you fail, but you are doomed if you don't try.
—BEVERLY SILLS

Davia Temin, president of Temin & Co. and former head of corporate marketing for General Electric Capital Service, remembers the exact moment she realized that "almost everything is negotiable, if you see it that way." She was raised in a middle-class family in Ohio and was taught as a girl to "follow the rules." She spent the early part of her life doing just that. When she got out of business school, she accepted her first job as assistant to the director of development at the Columbia Business School without really negotiating. She saw the offer as a choice, not a negotiation: You either took the job or you did not. It never crossed her mind that she could negotiate the offer.

While working at Columbia, however, she saw something that changed her view of the world. She had always assumed that when you applied to business school, you either got accepted or you didn't. If you didn't, you went to another business school or went on to do something else. That is what most people did. But a few students who were rejected came in to see the dean of admissions. They said something to the effect that, "I know you rejected my application, but I really want to go to Columbia Business School. What can I do to change your mind?" To Davia's amazement, the director of admissions did not send them away, but advised them to enroll in the School of General Studies and take four semesters of advanced calculus and statistics, "And if you get As in each of those courses," she would say, "I'll admit you." A handful of students actually took her up on her offer and were admitted. Davia suddenly realized that "way more things were negotiable than I had previously thought." So she decided to learn how to negotiate.

The biggest mistake women make is not to negotiate. Like Davia, many women look at situations in terms of decisions they have to make, not opportunities to negotiate. They either accept the offer or turn it down. There are many reasons why this happens, but often women simply fail to realize that they can question what is being offered and ask for something else. Successful women understand that almost everything is negotiable— although you do not want to negotiate everything. They know how to pick their battles. But when they choose to accept something without negotiating, it is a conscious decision. Remember, if you do not ask for what you want, you are unlikely to get it.

Ronna Lichtenberg is President of Clear Peak Communications and the author of *It's Not Business, It's Personal: The Nine Relationship Principles That Power Your Career*. As president of her own company and as a former senior vice president at Prudential Securities, she has negotiated major deals involving hundreds of thousands of dollars, yet the negotiation she is proudest of is having convinced a salesman at Neiman Marcus to sell her a pair of Manolo Blahnik shoes for $125.

While on vacation in San Francisco, she came across a pair of the designer's shoes in her size on sale at Neiman Marcus. She had the same pair in another color and loved them. While she could easily afford them, she couldn't justify spending $395, even on sale, for shoes she already had in another color. So she said to the salesman, "You know these are a size 7-AA. You are not going to be able to sell them to anyone else. It's right before Christmas, and you are going to mark them down again right after New Year's. So you can either take an imprint of my credit card now and send them to me after you take that second markdown, or I can walk out of here and you won't get a commission for selling me a pair of shoes." He walked away for a moment to think about her offer, then he came back, and took her credit card. Shortly after New Year's, she received a package in the mail from Neiman Marcus—a pair of Manolo Blahniks for $125.

Ronna negotiated this perfectly. She understood what motivated the salesman and was able to convince him that what she was proposing was in his interest as well as hers. But that is not why she told us about this transaction. She is proud of this negotiation because normally she would not even have thought of attempting it.

Women often fail to consider the possibility of negotiating even in circumstances when men routinely do. For instance, women, particularly young women, typically don't negotiate when they accept a new job. They see the offer as a choice that they can either accept or decline. Men, on the other hand, recognize these situations as opportunities to negotiate a significant increase in their compensation. (See Chapter 9).

Although one major advantage women bring to the bargaining table is their ability to develop relationships, this advantage too often becomes a disadvantage when women fail to negotiate out of fear that doing so will damage their relationship with the other person. Never underestimate the power of asking. You may not always get what you ask for, but, if you ask in the right way, you will rarely lose by trying. You will also be surprised at how often you get all or at least some of what you ask for.

＞－◇－○－◇－＜

At times, when I am negotiating, I remember a quote from hockey great Wayne Gretzky that my dad put up on my door when I was 12: "You miss 100 percent of the shots you don't take." Throughout my childhood, my father constantly told me that I could do anything I wanted and be whatever I wanted to be if I had the courage to go after it.

By the time I reached high school, that lesson had obviously taken hold. Without even thinking about it, I instinctively asked for what I wanted. For example, in eleventh grade, I got a history teacher to change my grade from a B to an A simply by asking. I had been more interested in my social life and in playing soccer than in studying that quarter, but I was not happy with the B. So I went to talk with the teacher who told me that I had just missed getting an A. Instead of accepting that answer, I asked him to give me the A and promised to work extra hard the next quarter. To my surprise, he said okay.

＞－◇－○－◇－＜

Sometimes the very thing you are afraid to ask for is something the people you are dealing with would welcome. Lisa Caputo, former Press Secretary to First Lady Hillary Clinton and now President of Citigroup's Women & Co., learned the importance of asking for what you want when she got to the White House. Earlier in her career, she had often allowed others to tell her what was going to happen. At the White House, she was put in a position where she had to negotiate with the press on a daily basis. "The more I negotiated, the more confidence I had to ask. The more times I was met with a favorable response, the more I realized not to be afraid to ask. Soon asking became a basic tenet of how I negotiated."

Shortly after she arrived at the White House, Lisa was able to put that insight to good use. She had barely had time to set up her office when television journalists began asking to interview the First Lady. Ultimately, the White House decided to give the first television interview to Katie Couric, who cohosts the NBC *Today Show* each morning. But Lisa wanted the first interview to be in evening prime time so it would reach the largest possible audience. She also wanted it to be an hour-long special. So she asked. NBC and Katie Couric were not only open to the idea, they loved it. So the interview aired as an hour-long NBC news special in prime time, and it proved to be a great ratings success.

Getting over the fear of asking is not enough. You also need to ask for more than you expect to get. To be a successful negotiator, you must set your expectations high. This does not mean beginning your negotiations by asking for something totally unrealistic. That will only damage your credibility and may even result in the other party terminating the discussion before it begins. In Chapter 3, you will learn how to anchor your offer— determining the range of reasonable possible outcomes to which the parties might agree and making your initial offer in a way that not only favors your position but is accepted by the other side as an appropriate starting point for the negotiations.

In general, even if you don't get everything you ask for, the more you ask for, the more you'll be given. If we know that, then why do most women ask for too little? In psychologist Patricia Farrell's view:

> Women sometimes don't realize that you don't start where you want to end. They really believe that the other person will do the right thing by them. Primarily this is what happens in families. It may also have to do with a lack of confidence, or it may result from their greater sense of fairness. They may be afraid of looking foolish. Some women feel that asking for more, at least if it is for themselves, would be "greedy."

Whatever your reason for not asking, you can't expect to get what you don't ask for, and, if you ask for too little, you can be sure that that's what you'll get.

The negotiating process requires compromise. In most negotiations, there is an expectation that where you start is not where you will finish. Therefore, most people would feel foolish if they simply gave you everything you asked for, no matter how reasonable your proposal. To feel good about the final agreement, most people require some give-and-take. If your initial offer is where you would actually like to end up, then you'll either fail to reach an agreement or you'll have to take less in the end. Otherwise, the other parties will not feel that they have been included in the process. This does not mean that you should treat negotiating as a game in which you manipulate the other side. Rather, when you are doing your preparation, determine the best result you could possibly hope for; what you realistically think you can accomplish; and your bottom line—the least you are willing to accept. Then, using the tools in this book, seek the best possible result. Even if you don't actually get everything you want, you will end up better off than if you had set your sights lower.

If carried out properly, there is something therapeutic about the negotiating process. Even though both sides don't get everything they want or, paradoxically perhaps, *because* they don't get everything they want, everyone walks away satisfied that they did the best that they could. When you ask for more than you expect and accept that negotiating requires give-and-take, you allow room for the process to work. This, in turn, increases the likelihood that you will not only get the things most important to you but that both sides will feel that the end result is fair.

NEGOTIATE FOR YOURSELF AS IF YOU WERE NEGOTIATING FOR SOMEONE ELSE

Everyone is valued in this world as he shows by his conduct that he wishes to be valued.
—JEAN DE LA BRUYERE

When Carol Raphael is negotiating on behalf of her organization, the Visiting Nurse Service of New York, she always tries to get the best deal she can. On the other hand, she admitted in her interview for this book that she might have gotten a better compensation package for herself the last time her contract was renewed. Instead, she asked the board or directors for what she thought was fair, and they agreed to give it to her.

Like many of the women we interviewed, Carol has a difficult time negotiating for herself. But she doesn't want to feel that she is being taken advantage of, so she would have no problem seeking a raise if she felt she was being paid significantly less than her peers at similar organizations. While we do not advocate pushing to get every last penny you could when you negotiate, there is nothing wrong with negotiating for yourself.

As psychologist Patricia Farrell notes, "Women find it much less difficult to negotiate on behalf of others. This places them in the role of caregiver, a role they feel very comfortable in." When it comes to negotiating for themselves, according to Dr. Farrell, women often feel "that they don't deserve what they are asking for." Moreover, because women tend to view things in the context of relationships, they take things personally. Asking for things for themselves becomes more difficult because if they are turned down, they see it as a personal rejection. Even women who are excellent negotiators may find it difficult to negotiate well on their own behalf.

Sometimes just recognizing that you have a tendency to put others' needs ahead of your own is enough to change your behavior. Randi Kahn, a Managing Director at Salomon Smith Barney who negotiates multi-million-dollar real estate deals for a living, recognizes that she has a hard time when it comes to negotiating for herself. Therefore, she compensates for it. She simply forces herself to push just as hard or harder when she is negotiating for herself. As a result, she has been able to succeed in the very male-dominated world of investment banking.

Dr. Farrell suggests that one way for a woman to overcome her reluctance to ask for things on her own behalf is to "take yourself outside yourself: See yourself as negotiating for someone else. Ask yourself what you would do if you were advocating for someone else." Before you begin, give yourself a little pep talk. Sit down and make a list of the reasons why you deserve what you are asking for.

If, however, after trying to negotiate for yourself using the techniques in this book you still cannot do so with the same forcefulness you would use on behalf of others, recognize that and take a different approach. For example, bring in someone else to encourage and reassure you that what you are asking for is appropriate.

Bonnie Stone, CEO of Women In Need, is an excellent negotiator when she is working on behalf of others. She recognizes, however, that she is not good at getting what she wants for herself. Sometimes she "has" to have something. She understands that this violates one of the key rules for successful negotiating—"Be willing to walk away"—so, when she has to negotiate for herself, she brings in other people to help her. For example, when she was looking to buy her first apartment in New York City, she fell in love with one particular apartment. She "had" to have it. Knowing herself, she asked her brother, who is an attorney, to help her negotiate the purchase. She wanted to offer the asking price rather than risk losing the apartment. Her brother advised her not to offer that much. Although her fear of losing the apartment was almost intolerable, she listened to him and offered a lower price. The next day the sellers called to accept her offer.

Many young girls are taught that if people care about you, they will give you what you want without your asking. That may be true for children, but as an adult, if you don't ask for it, you generally don't get it. Most people, even those who care about you, cannot read your mind. Let them know what you want. Our guess is that what you want is not only reasonable but also probably much less than you could actually get. Never be embarrassed to ask for what you want. Be as forceful an advocate for yourself as you would be if you were negotiating for someone else.

MASTER THE DETAILS, BUT BE FLEXIBLE AND NEVER LOSE SIGHT OF YOUR ULTIMATE GOAL

When one door closes, another opens. But we often look so regretfully upon the closed door that we don't see the one that has opened for us.
—ALEXANDER GRAHAM BELL

Most women are detail oriented. This can be a major strength, and often one reason why successful women have been able to get to where they are. They make sure that they are better prepared than the people with whom they are negotiating. Author and former CNN executive Gail Evans attributes this to the "game of knowledge" that girls learn while growing up. In school, they are rewarded "with good grades, parental approval, [and] teacher attention for being a good student, for doing their homework [and] for being prepared when called upon. They carry this training into adulthood." Dr. Patricia Farrell believes that women tend to overprepare because "they don't want to look foolish. Their sometimes-fragile sense of self is on the line. They don't feel comfortable working without a script."

Being better prepared than the people you are dealing with can give you a huge advantage. Preparation often enables women to get the respect they need to negotiate on a level playing field with men. Men are much less forgiving of women who make mistakes with the facts than they are with men under similar circumstances. Moreover, the better prepared you are, the more convincing you will be.

On the other hand, women sometimes get so caught up in the details that they lose sight of what they are trying to achieve. When you are trying to persuade someone to your point of view, it is important to focus on the details that are important to them. Edit your points. Just because you know something doesn't mean everyone needs to know it. If you share too much information, you lose your audience. Moreover, there is no need to argue over an issue just because you are more knowledgeable than someone else, especially if it doesn't move things along in the right direction. Even if the other side is incorrect, you need deal with the issue only if it makes a difference. Otherwise, you run the risk of alienating that person for no reason. Always remain focused on your real goal, which is to reach an agreement that satisfies your needs. Avoid getting so mired in the details that you risk losing the deal because you can't step back and see the big picture.

Terri Santisi, the Global Head of KPMG's Media and Entertainment Group, was brought into a negotiation that had stalled to see if she could break the stalemate. She was initially presented with several dozen issues that the other side wanted resolved in a certain way and her side had previously been unwilling to agree to. Terri approached the negotiations methodically and asked the other side to explain each issue. Over the next several months, she worked with the other side on each one, paying close attention to the details and trying to be as responsive as possible. By mastering the details, she was able to resolve some of the issues by showing them that they didn't have the facts right or didn't have all the facts. She resolved other issues by being creative or by compromising. As important as her mastery of the details was, it was even more important that she never lost sight of her ultimate objective: not only to do this deal but to do future deals with these individuals as well.

From the beginning, Terri knew that each side had only one or two points that were actual deal breakers—issues they had to have resolved in their favor or they would not agree to a deal. By keeping the deal breakers in mind, she was able to resolve the other points easily. She achieved her overall bottom-line goals and her objectives on the deal-breaker issues by making compromises, by granting concessions in one area in return for getting concessions in another, and by coming up with creative solutions that satisfied everyone's needs. In that way, she was able to craft an agreement that satisfied both sides rather than trying to demonstrate that her position on each point was superior to the one being put forth by her adversary. This is the most effective way to put your mastery of the details to use.

Sometimes, when we negotiate, we get so wrapped up in winning various negotiating points that we lose sight of the big picture. Before she came to New York, Jan Hopkins, television anchor for CNN's *Street Sweep,* was working at a television station in Cincinnati. When she got divorced and moved to New York, she ended up owning the condominium in Cincinnati. She wasn't sure if things would work out in New York, so she rented it out. When she decided to stay in New York, she hired a lawyer in Cincinnati to negotiate the sale of the condominium to her tenants, who were interested in purchasing it. The lawyer got a good offer from them, but he told her that he knew the market and that he thought he could get another thousand dollars from them. So she held out—and the tenants bought another condominium. Although her lawyer was extremely knowledgeable about how to value condominiums in that market, Jan allowed herself to lose sight of her goal: to sell her place in Cincinnati so she could buy a place in New York. Instead, it took her two more years to find a buyer, and even then she ended up selling it for less. "All over a thousand dollars," she says.

As with any generalization, though, there are exceptions. Not all women are adept at mastering details. That is why you must know yourself, so you can compensate for things you don't do well or don't want to do. Carol Evans, Publisher of Working Mother Media describes herself as a "big-picture person." She readily admits that she dislikes spending her time dealing with the details of a deal. Her strength lies in focusing on the end goal, so she tries to keep deals simple, and if a deal gets complex she brings in someone else to handle the details.

AVOIDING THE EMPATHY TRAP: BE EMPATHETIC, BUT NOT TOO EMPHATHETIC

If I am not for myself, who will be? But if I am only for myself what am I?

—ETHICS OF THE FATHER

Women tend to be better listeners than men and to more readily grasp the other side's position. As mentioned, they treat negotiations as a prelude to a continuing relationship. For that to occur, the other party has to walk away from the negotiations feeling good about what they have agreed to. Understanding how the other person perceives the situation is an important first step. Men tend to be more task oriented. They care about the other person's feelings only to the extent that those feelings are relevant to the successful conclusion of the negotiation at hand. Men negotiate, reach agreement, and move on to their next task.

Women seldom draw such strict boundaries between negotiations and relationships beyond the negotiations. For women, developing an enduring relationship can be as important as the outcome of the negotiations itself. Taking this long-term view can lead to great success as a negotiator. KPMG's Terri Santisi has what she calls her "Golden Rule of Negotiating":

> When you sit down at the table to negotiate, remember you are there because you want to have a continuing relationship with them. Once you walk away from the table, you are going to be in that relationship. Always keep that objective firmly in mind.

This view leads women to work to empower all the participants and to satisfy everyone's needs. As a result, women alternate between listening and contributing.

Men tend to look at the other person's position from their own perspective. They consider how they would react if they were in a similar situation. Women are better able to look at things from the other person's perspective, to understand how they actually see things. This ability to empathize is an advantage women bring to the table. Moreover, men instinctively feel that women are more understanding because they are used to seeing women in nurturing roles as mothers and wives. As a result, they are more willing to trust and open up to women. If you can get men to open up, they will provide you with all the information you need to understand their point of view, which in turn will cause them to perceive you as understanding their needs. Being able to show that you understand and thereby acknowledge the validity of someone else's position is an extremely effective way of getting them to understand and accommodate your position.

However, women sometimes fall into the trap of being too empathetic. According to Dr. Farrell:

> Women are able to see things from another person's point of view. They put themselves in the other person's shoes. They have been raised to do that. That is how they get hurt. They know how they would feel and can feel the hurt they cause. They instinctively want to fix it, but once others realize that, they can use it to get what they want.

Men are not above using empathetic feelings to gain an advantage. A male business student in one of my classes described his experience negotiating against his female classmates as follows:

> In several cases, if the other party was a female, I was able to actually gain an advantage by appealing to her emotional side. I used sincerity in a charming manner to try building a greater degree of trust. After this trust was established, it was much easier to use other tactics, such as bluffing.

Some people will take advantage of your empathy if you let them.

Understanding the other side's position is not the same thing as allowing yourself to be convinced that their position should prevail, especially if that would work to your detriment. Empathy is about understanding their needs, not necessarily about giving them what they want. Recognizing others' interests will enable you to fashion a result that meets everyone's needs. But don't let empathy keep you from protecting your own interests. Lynne Newsome, a highly regarded New Jersey divorce lawyer, frequently finds her female clients arguing with her that their soon-to-be ex-husbands "can't afford this" or "shouldn't have to do that." Realistically understanding a divorcing spouse's concerns can facilitate a fair settlement, but focusing on his needs to your detriment will not. We call this the "empathy trap": Not only do you understand what is important to the person you are negotiating with, but you actually let them convince you that their needs are more important than yours.

Author and former CNN executive Gail Evans recalls that when she was in her twenties she fell into an empathy trap that cost her a prestigious fellowship. She had been working at the White House when she decided to apply for a fellowship at an Ivy League university and was invited for an interview. When she arrived at the appointed time, she was greeted by the proverbial three "old white male professors" who invited her to sit down, and proceeded to interrogate her. She felt she was doing pretty well until one professor said, "You know that it costs us $10,000 a year to fund a fellow. What we expect in return is that you will use what you learn to give back to the community through years of public service. How do we know that you won't accept this fellowship, work for a year or two, and then just get married and have children?" Gail went home and thought about what he had said. Ten thousand dollars was a lot of money in those days, and Gail did intend to get married and have children eventually. She also thought that she might want to stay home and raise them. So she withdrew her application.

As ridiculous as this example seems today, women do the same thing in other contexts all the time when they let their notions of fairness and empathy stand in the way of their getting what they want. The things you want are no less important than what your husband, your children, your boss, or your clients want. Sometimes you can collaborate to find a solution that satisfies everyone's needs. At other times, you can convince them that what you want is fair and appropriate and in their interest as well. You can also create different ways to approach the problem if you think it will help you achieve your objectives. Use your empathy to understand the other person's needs, but never lose sight of your own.

BE WILLING TO SAY NO, BUT DON'T BE TOO WILLING TO ACCEPT NO FOR AN ANSWER

There's a point where you just have to say no, whether it's with kids or in business.
— JACK WELCH

Susanna Hoffs, of the Bangles, blames the group's breakup in the late 1980s on their inability to say no to going out on tour. She did not want to go on tour. Neither did the other members of the band. They were tired. What they really needed was a rest. But their manager, their record company, their fans, and just about everyone else wanted them to go on tour. So they did. During the tour, tensions mounted. The situation deteriorated so badly that they canceled the tour abruptly and the band split up. Susanna always blamed the stress of that final tour for the breakup, so, when they decided to put the band back together ten years later, the one thing they all agreed on was that if any one of them felt uncomfortable about doing something, they would all say no to it.

"No" is the most powerful word in negotiating, but many women have difficulty saying it. They want to keep everyone happy. They want to avoid conflict. They want to be liked. They want to please. Psychologist Patricia Farrell attributes women's reluctance to say no to the importance they place on relationships:

> Women are eager to maintain good relationships. They have a difficult time believing that if there is a negative outcome, it won't have a negative effect on the relationship. A woman would rather walk away with less than she could have gotten if she believes it will maintain the relationship.

To be a good negotiator, you must be able to say no. You can say it without damaging your relationship with the other party. It all depends on how you say it. When you say no it must be firm, and it must be credible. Choosing the right words will make both easier.

There are a lot of ways to say no. For example, you might say, "Tom, I really want to work with you on this, but I can't agree to what you are suggesting. How about…" or "Tom, I don't think that will work because…. Have you considered…?" Of course, it helps if you can provide sound reasons why you are saying no. Sometimes, though, you won't be able to articulate a good reason. You simply do not want to agree to whatever is being asked of you, be it going out on a date, volunteering to run the PTA dance, or discounting the price of your services. In those instances, just say no—nicely, politely, and firmly.

When you say no, particularly when you are dealing with men, tone is also important. Women are often most effective when they can convey the message with quiet conviction. You do not have to say no loudly to say it effectively. You do not want to appear strident, but rather firm and unwavering. Although your bottom line must remain firm, you also want to remain flexible in how you get there.

>—⊷•○•⊶—<

> Being able to say no was critical in my negotiating a good price for the townhouse I recently purchased. I was looking to buy a house in Baltimore. On the very first day it came on the market, I came across a three-story, nineteenth-century townhouse. I fell in love with it. I knew, though, that if I had to I could walk away from the deal. The sellers had the house listed at $220,000. The market for houses in downtown Baltimore had been hot, with

buyers frequently getting into bidding wars and ending up paying more than the seller's initial asking price. Luckily, the market had begun to cool. I felt that the asking price was too high, so I offered $195,000. I knew that was low, but not out of the ballpark. I expected the sellers to turn down the offer, but I hoped they would come back with a reasonable counter-offer. Instead, they simply rejected it out of hand and refused to even make a counter-offer. They asked me to come back with a "more reasonable" offer, but I refused.

Because the house had literally just come on the market, I knew that the sellers had visions of competing buyers bidding up the price beyond their asking price and they were not psychologically ready to accept anything less. So I decided to let some time pass, and I hoped no one would make a better offer. I told the sellers that I wouldn't make another offer but would consider a counter-offer from them if they changed their mind before I found something else. Then, making sure they knew that I was continuing to look at other houses, I waited. The housing market continued to soften, and the sellers did not get any other offers. About two weeks later, they made a counter-offer of $215,000. I responded by offering $205,000, and they accepted. Because I had said no in a way that kept the door open to further negotiations, I was able to buy the house for $15,000 less than the sellers were originally willing to accept.

Jessica's home-buying experience demonstrates that saying no may also be a matter of timing. In any negotiation, sometimes it may be too soon to say yes to something. As discussed earlier, bargaining of any kind requires give-and-take. The other side expects you to make concessions. If you don't offer concessions, people think that you are not considering their needs. But if you grant concessions too readily, the other side will not value them. So before you can say yes sometimes you have to first say no.

Conversely, when someone tells you no, it is not necessarily the end of the discussion. Rather, it is an opportunity to find out what you must do to get them to say yes. The most difficult person to sell to is the one who listens politely to what you have to say, thanks you, and just doesn't buy. Because these prospects never say no, it is impossible to get them to say yes. When they say no, at least you have the opportunity to find out why. In sales training, this is called "eliciting objections." Once you understand someone's objections, you can use one or more of the *convince, collaborate,* and *create* approaches we discuss throughout the book to address them.

Moreover, just because one person says no doesn't mean that you can't ask someone else. Maybe you are just not asking the right person. Sometimes persistence is your most important negotiating tool. Donna Lagani, Publishing Director for the Cosmopolitan Group, which publishes *Cosmopolitan* and *CosmoGirl,* offers sound advice, "Never take no from someone who cannot say yes."

Saying no is not personal. It has nothing to do with you or your relationship with the person with whom you are negotiating. It is just part of the negotiating process. Saying no is one way to exchange information about your needs. Looked at that way, saying no becomes a lot easier, as does dealing with no when someone says it to you.

DON'T TAKE IT PERSONALLY: IT'S ALL RIGHT TO FEEL EMOTIONS WHEN YOU NEGOTIATE, AS LONG AS YOU DON'T NEGOTIATE EMOTIONALLY

There is no crying in baseball.
—TOM HANKS IN *A LEAGUE OF THEIR OWN*

In a recent episode of the HBO television series *Sex and the City,* Kim Catrell's character, Samantha, is trying to convince a hotel owner to hire her to handle his public relations work. He infuriates her by telling her that, although she is the best qualified person to do the work, he is not going to hire her because she slept with his accountant and it would be "uncomfortable."

Samantha is so angry and hurt that she is on the verge of tears. She immediately gets up and leaves. She barely makes it to the elevator, where, alone, she breaks down and cries. The next day the hotel owner calls to offer her the job because she has "balls."

To negotiate well, you have to be able to step back and see the big picture. That means maintaining your emotional objectivity. Good negotiators "lose their cool" only for effect.

One common negotiating mistake women make is to let their emotions affect the way they negotiate. We have all made that mistake at one time or another. Negotiating can bring out a variety of emotions ranging from anger to becoming overly excited about the prospect of getting something that you want. It is normal to feel emotions when you negotiate, but when you are in that state of mind you cannot negotiate effectively, and it is best not to try. Tell the other party that you have an appointment, and schedule another meeting for a later date. Take a break to get a bite to eat, or get a cup of coffee. If you just need a few moments to regain your composure, go to the ladies room. It is one place where a man won't be able to follow you. The important thing is to give yourself enough time to be able to negotiate unemotionally when you return.

Dee Soder, Ph.D., founder and Managing Partner of The CEO Perspective Group and an excellent negotiator, describes one instance in which waiting until she was in a better frame of mind to negotiate might have facilitated a more productive negotiation later on. It was late in the day, and she was tired. Her staff had been trying for months to get a DSL line correctly installed in her office. She finally called the company herself and received a call back near the end of the day. The person who called was not the person she had tried to reach and was not particularly helpful. Rather than calling back later, as she recognizes she should have done, she continued with the call and "vented" about all the problems she had been having with the company. The discussion was totally unproductive. Nothing got resolved. As a result, it took her staff three more months and numerous additional calls to get the DSL line installed properly.

AVOID NEGOTIATING WHEN YOU ARE TOO:

D istracted

I rritated

S tressed

T ired

R attled

A ngry

C onfused

T earful

E xcited

D istraught

Not only should you not let your emotions affect how you negotiate; it is also important not to let them show, especially when you are negotiating with men. Women show their emotions differently than men do. This results from the way they are raised. Psychologist Patricia Farrell describes it this way:

> Men get angry. Women take things personally. When they are growing up, girls are allowed to be emotional. Girls can cry. Boys can't. For a girl, being upset, being emotional, is acceptable. Because we are talking about relationships, for women it's always personal.

When you are negotiating, though, particularly in business, emotional displays can hurt. If a man screams, he is forgiven because he is considered a tough guy who has merely lost his temper. As previously discussed, a woman who screams is considered a "bitch" that cannot control herself. If a man cries, he is looked at as compassionate—as long as it doesn't happen too often or at a time when he is expected to be in control. But a woman who cries is branded "overly emotional." This may not be fair, but, at least until we become more enlightened as a society, it is the reality.

Men like to think of themselves as being rational at all times. They want to believe that they negotiate dispassionately. Most men would say that they prefer to deal with others who negotiate that way as well. Although while, in fact, men often let their emotions affect the way they negotiate, they always try to appear "cool under fire" regardless of their real feelings. Similarly, even if you are excited or someone has managed to "get to you," don't show it. This takes practice. Carolyn Wall, the former Publisher of *Newsweek* told us, "One of the hardest things for me is to cap the emotions I might feel, particularly if I am excited [about a deal]. So I keep focused on not showing emotion. If I can't be flat, at least, I try to be inscrutable."

Crying is the emotional display that men most dread. It can be deadly for a woman in the business context. *The Wall Street Journal* reported that Deborah Hopkins, who had been lured away from Boeing to join Lucent as CFO, lost critical support from the board of directors after she broke down in tears following tough questioning about a presentation she had just given. The fact that a member of the board of directors would mention the incident to a reporter only points up how truly damaging an emotional display can be for a woman. To gain and keep the respect you need to negotiate on an equal footing with men in business, leave the room before you cry.

When men negotiate with you, they may fail to treat you with the respect you deserve. They may scream at you or belittle you. Whether this behavior is a tactic to throw you off, or is unintentional, there are ways to effectively deal with it. One way is to ignore it, as Cathy Harbin does. As general manager of the two world-class golf courses at the World Golf Village, where the PGA's Golf Hall of Fame is located, Cathy is a rarity in the world of golf. She frequently encounters men who, when she negotiates with them, start out by treating her as if she were their wife or daughter. Some of them call her "sweetie" or "darling." She doesn't get upset or angry. As she says, "They don't necessarily mean it that way, and even if they do, what good does it do to get offended by it?" She ignores it and goes on with her business. She just keeps being herself until they realize they have to speak to her in a different way.

You can also deal with efforts to intimidate you by refusing to continue until they cease. Another option is to openly discuss what the other person is doing ("Let's talk about why you think you can intimidate me by yelling"). Or you could use humor to defuse the situation ("Is it my turn to scream yet?") One thing you should not do, though, is become angry or upset, unless you are doing it for effect.

Whenever Davia Temin, President of Temin & Co., feels like yelling at someone with whom she is negotiating, she recalls advice her father gave her. He used to say, "If I were rich, I would build a soundproof room. Then whenever I got upset I could go there, break cheap china and when I calmed down I could go out and deal with things." Then she takes a mental "china break." She doesn't lose her temper. Instead she intentionally tries to match her style to that of the person she is dealing with. If he gets tough, she gets tough back. If he screams, she gets "quietly tough" and "just keeps coming back at him." But she doesn't yell. In Davia's words, "When women yell, they come across as whiny or bitchy, and that doesn't work."

Although screaming, yelling, and carrying on simply does not work for women most of the time, even that rule has exceptions. Davia had a client who always yelled. All the other women at her firm put up with him and didn't say anything, but Davia would not tolerate it, even from an important client. She tried everything to get him to behave differently. She brought it to his attention; she asked him not to do it; she told him to stop. Nothing worked. Finally, after much thought, one day she yelled back at him. It worked. He respected that and he stopped yelling at her staff. When all else fails, you may have to raise your voice to be effective, but only when all else fails and only for effect. Lisa Hall, COO of Oxygen Media, also believes that you should raise your voice only as a last resort and never out of anger. "Screaming is inappropriate for women, except when it isn't." Then she adds, "but no whining, under any circumstances."

It's easy to get caught up in the moment and lose the emotional objectivity necessary to negotiate well. If you do, you will make mistakes. Not only avoid getting angry but also prevent yourself from becoming committed to the outcome. Sometimes we get so excited about an opportunity that we forget to ask all the right questions. Cathy Black, President of Hearst Magazines, recalls how Al Neuharth, then Chairman of media company Gannett and creator of *USA Today*, tried several times to get her to work for him, but she wasn't interested in any of the jobs he spoke to her about. Then one day he called and said, "I think I found a job for you. How would you like to be President of *USA Today*?" She couldn't believe it. That was a job she really wanted. They agreed on the money and the basic employment terms. Then she accepted the job. In her excitement, though, she failed to ask exactly what her responsibilities would be or who would report to her. That was a mistake. She was attending a luncheon to announce her appointment, and right before they made the announcement, a senior executive came up to her, congratulated her, and then added, "I just want to let you know, I had dinner with Neuharth yesterday, and he told me I don't report to you." It took her three months to rectify the reporting relationship.

Whenever Katie Blackburn, an Executive Vice President for the Cincinnati Bengals football team, finds herself getting too excited about the prospect of signing a player with whom she is negotiating a contract, she asks herself, "What would happen if we don't get this guy? What are our options?" This allows her to put things back in perspective. It helps her to walk away if she cannot convince the player to sign after she has made him her best offer.

Negotiating is not personal. It's about getting what you want. The people with whom you are negotiating have the same objective. It's fine to like the people on the other side, but don't feel you have to reach an agreement because of your relationship with them. Relationships are only one part of the bargaining equation. Unless you have misled the other person about your intentions, the relationship is not likely to suffer if you decline the offer, particularly if you state your reasons for doing so. In the end, maintaining emotional objectivity means being able to walk away from an agreement that is not in your best interest.

GOOD GIRLS DON'T, BUT SUCCESSFUL WOMEN DO: DON'T BE AFRAID TO BREAK THE RULES

A ship in port is safe, but that is not what ships are for.
—REAR ADMIRAL GRACE MURRAY HOPPERS

Carole Cooper is an owner/agent at N.S. Bienstock, Inc. She represents television personalities such as Fox's Bill O'Reilly, CBS's Jack Ford, and NBC's Soledad O'Brien. When she graduated from college, she had no real work experience. But she did have a burning desire to work in the entertainment business, so she got an interview at MPO, at that time the largest commercial production company in the country. They were looking for an assistant who could type and take shorthand. Although Carole could type a little, she didn't know any shorthand. Nonetheless, she told them "I could do everything." Luckily, they didn't test her, so she got the job. About two weeks later, her boss called her in and asked her to take a letter. She took some notes, typed up a letter, and put it in his inbox for him to sign. Later that day, he called her into his office, looked straight at her, and asked, "So you take shorthand?" She replied, "I write a good letter." He laughed and said, "I like you. You're gutsy. We'll try it this way." She worked for him for four years, and when he left MPO he took her with him, taught her the business, and helped her become a producer. None of that would have occurred had she listened when she was told shorthand was required for the position.

We often do things either because someone has told us that's how we ought to do them, or because they have been done that way in the past. This mind-set is limiting. When you negotiate, your ability to be creative is not only unlimited, as we discuss in Chapter 5, it is one of the three pillars upon which successful negotiating is based. The only real limitations when you negotiate are those you impose on yourself.

Vivian Eyre, a career consultant and the President of Partners for Women's Growth, frequently encounters women who are held back by being too "rules oriented." The following story about a client, which I recount in my earlier book, *Get More Money on Your Next Job,* illustrates this problem.

Her client had been hired by a publishing company to head a new imprint. When she was hired, her compensation package, in line with the company's compensation practices, was weighted more heavily toward base salary than bonus. Through her talent and hard work, she was able to increase revenues by more than 30 percent in her first year. Her superior and her peers recognized her accomplishments, yet the closer she got to bonus time, the more dissatisfied she became. Even if she were awarded the maximum bonus for which she was eligible, it would clearly be inadequate in light of what she had accomplished. When she came to Vivian, she was ready to leave her job because of the bonus situation. Vivian suggested that she explain to her boss how she felt, and, in light of her performance, ask him to increase her bonus. Her client did not feel that she could do that because of the way the bonus plan was structured, but after a little coaching from Vivian, she went to her boss and negotiated a bigger bonus. Before coming to see Vivian, she was ready to leave a job she liked and did well. She had never seriously considered trying to renegotiate her bonus because she had let herself be intimidated by what she understood "the rules" to be.

If you are willing to take risks, you can sometimes get things you could not otherwise get. Good negotiators take calculated risks—risks that they believe are more likely than not to help them achieve their goals. They weigh the likelihood that their strategy will succeed against the consequences if it does not, and then decide whether it makes sense to proceed in that fashion.

Most young girls are socialized to follow the rules and to avoid taking risks. They are rewarded for respecting authority. They are taught to strive for perfection. Girls are constantly bombarded by images of physical perfection and told that they should try to emulate them. They are expected to be well behaved at all times and to always display good manners. Phrases like "perfect wife," "perfect mother," and "perfect 10" are thrown up at them. These are all unattainable goals, but the fear of failing to live up to those ideals and of making mistakes encourages women to play it safe.

Boys are not so burdened. No one expects them to be perfect. After all, "Boys will be boys." Boys are allowed to be wild. They are taught to be adventurous. They try new things, and when they screw up they make a joke out of it. Boys are encouraged by each other to take risks: to climb higher, to go where they shouldn't, to show off, and to risk getting in trouble. In fact, their peers reward them for breaking rules and not getting caught.

In negotiating, however, the only rule is there are no rules unless all the parties agree on them. When you negotiate, you can create the rules. You do not have to play by someone else's rules. You can break every rule but one: Never lie when negotiating, because if you get caught you will lose all credibility. You can, however, decide how best to structure your message—what you want to emphasize, how you want to present it, and what you choose to omit—as long as what you actually say is accurate. This is part of the art of convincing.

Creating is about changing the rules, taking calculated risks, and doing the unexpected. If playing by the rules won't get you where you want to go, change them, break them, or change the game.

LIGHTEN UP: A LITTLE HUMOR GOES A LONG WAY

The most wasted day is that in which we have not laughed.
—CHAMFORT

After she left Chanel, Kitty D'Alessio found herself negotiating with Henry Kravis, an investment banker who made billions through leveraged buyouts in the 1980s, about the possibility of running a business with his then wife, designer Carolyn Roehm. When Henry, a tough negotiator, asked Kitty how much she wanted to come work for him, she didn't know what to ask for. So she said, "A million dollars." Immediately, she knew she had asked for too much. His eyes narrowed, his body tensed, and he erupted, "You're nuts!" Without missing a beat, she replied, "Nice try, wasn't it?" He laughed and eventually agreed to a very generous compensation package for her.

In every negotiation, there are critical moments when things can go one of two ways: well or not so well. You may be having a serious disagreement, or the person with whom you are talking may be taking an unreasonable position. Tension fills the room. It looks as if everything is about to fall apart. Then someone says something funny, and the moment passes.

The purpose of using humor when you negotiate is not just to get a laugh but also to ease tension. Having a sense of humor makes people want to be around you. Humor can help you to connect with someone on a personal level and show that person another side of you. It can help you to develop a relationship. But you have to use it at the right time, and in an appropriate way. You never want to use it to put someone down. That will only make it harder to reach an agreement. Author and consultant Jean Hollands suggests using self-deprecating humor:

> Humor can help you out of everything, if you can lighten up and make fun of yourself. But Bully Broads tend to use humor sarcastically. That doesn't work. Although men can sometimes get away with sarcasm, when a woman does it the recipient, particularly if he is a male, is rendered impotent and he then doesn't want to help you

That is exactly what you want to avoid.

When someone makes you an offer that is much too low, it usually stops the negotiation cold. You are not going to make a counter-offer because doing so would be tantamount to accepting the offer as legitimate. (See discussion on Anchoring at pp. 75–81.) You could simply refuse to negotiate any further and insist that the other party give you a reasonable offer. That might, however be the end of the discussion. Or you could reply with humor. For example, when I was practicing law and an opposing lawyer would offer to settle a case for a million dollars, which seemed to occur whenever they didn't know where to begin, I would reply in a joking manner, "Perhaps if you pay me a million dollars I would agree to settle." And then I would say something like, "Maybe next time we do this, we can both try to be serious." Humor allowed the negotiation to go forward by giving the other side a chance to make a more realistic offer without losing face.

Humor can also be used to make a point. Actress Christine Baranski was backstage waiting to audition for a Neil Simon play. Manny Azenburg, the producer, came over to her and said, "You know, you can have this part if you want. Neil is crazy about you." Instead of "Thank you," the first words out of her mouth were, "You know, Christmas is a deal breaker." He laughed, which was what she intended. But she quickly added, "No, it really is." Being able to spend time with her children is important to Christine, but when you tell someone that something is not negotiable, you are taking a tough position. It helps if you can make the other side laugh while you are delivering that message.

Humor also works particularly well when you are negotiating with family members. Nancy Erica Smith, a prominent employment attorney with the law firm of Smith and Mullin, practices law with her husband Neil. He has always wanted to buy a Mercedes. If she told him that she didn't want him to get one, though, he would get defensive and angry. Then he would probably go right out and buy one. Instead she uses humor to make her point. Nancy has been known to remark to him when he mentions that he is thinking about buying a Mercedes: "Why don't you just get a license plate that says 'Midlife Crisis.' It's cheaper." This has been going on for years, and he still drives a jeep.

Humor works for Nancy with her children as well. Her son likes comic books. Nancy thinks they are sexist and violent, but she doesn't tell him he can't read them. Instead, she reads them with him and makes her point with humor. If she comes across a female character in a particularly revealing outfit she might say, "That's a nice outfit. Would you like me to wear something like that?"

It never hurts to have a sense of humor. Women often think they won't be taken seriously if they joke around. However, most women run a bigger risk of being perceived as humorless. Laughing is less about the joke than it is about the relationship. Sometimes you have to be serious, but, used properly, a little humor can break the tension and soften a tough position. Not everyone is funny, though; some people couldn't tell a joke if their life depended on it. Yet you can still show that you have a sense of humor by laughing when other people say something funny. Sometimes it pays to laugh, or at least smile, even if a joke isn't particularly funny. After all, you laugh at the jokes your young children and grandchildren tell you whether they are funny or not. It shows you care. The same is true in negotiating. Laughing is a way to make a connection whether you are telling a joke or just listening to one.

ACCEPT HUMAN NATURE, DON'T FIGHT IT

Human nature will not change.
—ABRAHAM LINCOLN

When you negotiate, you must take into consideration the other party's biases. Your job is not to change the people with whom you are dealing. You couldn't even if you wanted to. Your job is to understand them so you can figure out how best to achieve your objectives. One aspect of preparing your negotiating strategy is to take into consideration the biases of your intended audience so that you can determine whether you are the best person to handle the negotiation. This requires knowing yourself as well as knowing the people you are dealing with. That self-awareness will help you to figure out what will play best with the other side, not only in term of arguments but also who should deliver them.

For example, if you're negotiating with a man who appears to be biased, recognize that and take advantage of it. If you learn that he is uncomfortable negotiating with a woman and is more likely to acquiesce to avoid prolonging the situation, take advantage of that. If, as is sometimes the case, he is going to fight tooth and nail to avoid any perception of being out-negotiated by a woman, either figure out how to make him comfortable negotiating with you or bring in another man to negotiate for you. If you decide to bring in someone else, do so without appearing weak. Do this by bringing in someone who is recognized as having some special expertise that is relevant to what is being discussed. You can also take yourself out of negotiations by claiming to have other, more important, obligations. To do that, though, you should actually be involved in something more important, in case someone bothers to check out your reason.

When G. G. Michelson, formerly the Senior Vice President for External Affairs for R. H. Macy & Co., Inc., was a young labor negotiator, she was thrown into a negotiation with the president of a Teamster Union local. She had never dealt with him before, and he obviously believed that because she was a young woman she couldn't possibly have any authority. He wouldn't negotiate seriously with her. Recognizing that she wasn't getting anywhere, G. G. asked her boss, a man, to take over the negotiations. In hindsight, she believes that, if she had gotten to know the union leader and he had gotten to know her ahead of time, she could have changed the situation. But in the absence of a relationship, there was no way he would negotiate with a 20-year-old woman.

Women negotiators are often underestimated, particularly if they are young. Sometimes you can use that to your advantage. One of the most effective female lawyers I know was able to take apart an older male attorney by saying at the start of the negotiations that she hoped he wouldn't take advantage of her inexperience and would make her a fair offer. When he did, she treated his offer as the starting point and began to negotiate from there.

You can often take advantage of being underestimated by men by offering to do the first draft of any agreement. Men will usually acquiesce to such an offer and may even welcome the fact that they do not have to do the work. As any lawyer will tell you, the person who drafts the documents has a major advantage because you get to deal with the issues that have not been specifically addressed in a manner favorable to you, as long as you are consistent with what has actually been agreed to. The other side will then have to negotiate changes to what you have already drafted.

Most men are naturally competitive when they negotiate. To be successful with them, you either have to put them at ease or to take advantage of their competitiveness. Men can get so wrapped up in the game aspect of negotiations that they sometimes lose sight of what they are trying to achieve. What is important to them is winning. If you find yourself in that situation, you can let them think they are winning as long as you get what you want. You can do this by artfully using concessions. Let them believe that you want one thing when in fact there is something else more important to you. This will allow you to concede the first point to get an agreement on the latter. This can be more effective than going head-to-head with a male counterpart who places more importance on not appearing to lose to a woman than to actually reaching agreement. One of the women we interviewed went so far as to say that "when you negotiate with men you need to start higher than with women because they need to negotiate more. That way they can be heroes."

><->-O-<+><

Age can also play an important role in how you negotiate. When you are dealing with someone older or in a more powerful position, sometimes the best way to get what you want is by asking for advice or assistance. This approach can be particularly effective if you have a relationship with the person. When it comes to dealing with your parents, though, you may never succeed in getting them to treat you as an equal regardless of your age. Your parents always believe that, due to their greater experience, they know best. I even see this when my parents interact with their parents. Bosses or older, more experienced people in business may also treat you that way. You can't change the way they treat you, but you can make it work for you by approaching them seeking advice.

When I was deciding where to live after college, I approached my father about moving to Baltimore instead of to New York City. At first he hated the idea because I would still be living far away, and, after four years of seeing me only once every few months, he was hoping I would move to New York. I explained some of the advantages to living in Baltimore. I mentioned that the year before a friend had bought a townhouse as an investment in the area where I was considering living and had done very well with it. I know he is always interested in investment ideas, so I asked for his advice. Although I started out hoping he might give me a loan, we ended up deciding to buy the house together. He would put up the down payment, and I would fix up and maintain the house, and with a roommate, I would pay the mortgage and upkeep. When we sold the place, I would pay back the down payment and we would split the profits. He gets a good investment. I get a nice place to live and growing equity in a house.

Because I approached my father seeking advice rather than asking for a loan or for him to cosign for one, our discussions were a lot easier. Moreover, the solution we developed worked better for both of us than what I initially had in mind. We still debate whose idea it actually was to buy the house together. My dad is convinced that it was his. The one thing, though, that cannot be debated is that the best approach for me to take with him was to seek his advice.

>-+-+>-O-<+-+-<

No discussion of negotiating would be complete if we did not mention the basic human element of sex. Particularly for young women, sexual attraction can play a role in negotiating. In your personal life, it obviously will, but attractiveness can help you when you are negotiating with a man in a business setting. Just being a woman can be an advantage at times. Studies have shown that men are more likely to return a phone message or voicemail from a woman they do not know than one from a man. But using sex when you are negotiating, particularly in a business setting, can be very dangerous. Although being flirtatious may help you initially, it sets the wrong tone.

When Anna Lloyd, President and Executive Director of The Committee of 200, an organization of prominent women entrepreneurs and corporate leaders, was young, she soon became aware that in dealing with men, particularly older men, there was often an element of sexual attraction. As a young woman, she used flirtatiousness to her advantage. But as she got older and gained more confidence in her own abilities, she realized that flirting prevented her from developing the type of relationship she needed to deal with men as equals. Anna describes an incident when she was a young woman working in politics in which, instead of preparing, she thought she could charm a male colleague into agreeing to what she wanted. She was unsuccessful because she had not done her homework. To make matters worse, the colleague put her in the awkward position of suggesting that he might reconsider his position if they were to go out socially. She of course declined his invitation. Her experience, which has happened to many other young women even when they do nothing to encourage it, points out the dangers of using sex in negotiating. If you use your sexuality when you negotiate, you create an expectation that the flirtation will continue—and that is usually not your intention.

3

Convince
Changing the Way Others
See Things

To get what you want in life, you must often persuade others to
do things that they might not initially be inclined to do. This
requires convincing them that what you are proposing is in their
interest as well as in yours. Sometimes your efforts to convince
them will require giving them something in return. You may
even have to persuade them that what you are offering is something that they should want. In essence, as, Cosmopolitan Group
Publishing Director Donna Lagani states: "Negotiating is selling." Certainly, you are selling when you seek to convince others
to agree to what you are proposing.

Convince is the art of persuasion. It can be broken down into
three basic elements: listening, questioning, and delivering your
message. While the give-and-take of negotiating can be considered a fourth element, treating it that way makes many women

uncomfortable. Dealt with separately, women sometimes view the give-and-take of negotiating as moves and countermoves, a disingenuous process that can be inconsistent with the value they place on developing relationships. Therefore, we prefer to include the give-and-take of negotiating as part of how you deliver your message. It is just one of many ways to adjust your message in response to the feedback you receive from those with whom you are negotiating. Most women find it easier to incorporate concessions into their style of persuasion than to treat them as a bargaining tactic, where the other side may misconstrue any offer of an accommodation as weakness.

LISTENING

Negotiating is a dialogue, not a monologue. To persuade, you must first listen. If you listen, people will tell you exactly what to do to persuade them. Not only will you obtain critical information, but when others feel that you are listening to them, they become more open to listening to you. As Claire Irving, a principal in Investigative Consultants, LLC, a private investigation firm that specializes in investigating white-collar crime, puts it: "Three-quarters of negotiating is just listening."

When Claire was a Managing Director of Kroll Investigations, one of the largest private investigating firms in the country, she was given the unenviable task of trying to collect more than $4 million in outstanding bills, all of them several years old. Yet she was able to negotiate payment of $3.98 million, approximately 98 percent of those outstanding bills, simply by asking the right questions and listening to the answers. All she did was call the clients who were in arrears to find out why they hadn't paid. In most cases, the clients told her that Kroll had done something wrong or had promised to do something but hadn't followed through. By listening and allowing the clients to feel that they had been heard, in almost every case she was able to negotiate an agreement to pay. Sometimes she agreed to accept a slightly reduced payment; sometimes she allowed clients to pay over time; and sometimes she arranged for her firm to do what they had failed to do in the first place.

Many women think of negotiating as arguing, screaming, and haggling. Lisa Hall, Chief Operating Officer of Oxygen Media, understands, as do most successful women, that it is not. She says that some men in the entertainment industry like to scream and yell when they don't get their way, but if you don't let it intimidate you, screaming is not effective at all. Not only does she not let it intimidate her, she views such carrying-on as giving her an advantage: "When I am listening and they're screaming I will always win. Because if you are scream-ing, you're not listening. You need to listen to win."

When it comes to listening, most women have an advantage over men. They may not be trained to negotiate as they grow up, but they do learn how to listen. Girls, even today, are expected to figure out what people want and need without being told. They hone this skill watching younger siblings and babysitting. Mothers not only have to listen to their children but also anticipate their needs even before they learn to speak. Successful marriages depend on being able to communicate well, and it is typically the listening skills that the woman brings to the relationship that facilitates that communication. Cathleen Black, President of Hearst Magazines, believes, as do many of the women we interviewed, that:

> Women are better listeners. We didn't grow up in a hierarchical alignment of authority and decision making. We are open to hearing different opinions before making a decision. That does not mean we won't make tough decisions, but we try to get "buy in" by involving others in the decision.

That is an effective way to negotiate. I have learned in my years as a human resources executive and as a parent that people often think they aren't being heard. We all have a need to be heard. It validates us. It is at the heart of any relationship, whether professional or personal. Many times, all we really want is for someone to listen to us and acknowledge our point of view.

As the head of human resources at several companies, I have had the difficult task of firing people. This is a very delicate negotiation. The company wants terminated employees to exit quietly, without litigation. Employees want to be treated fairly and to receive a fair severance package. For many people, the most important thing is to be allowed to have their say. They want to be heard. People want their "day in court." If you don't give it to them, that is where you are likely to end up.

To communicate with your children, you also need to hear them and to acknowledge their feelings. Often just making an effort to understand their point of view is enough, even if you disagree with them and, in the end, don't allow them to do what they want. The same is true in virtually every type of negotiation. If you want others to be open to listening to you, they must feel that you are listening to them.

Listening does not mean agreeing, nor does acknowledging that you understand what someone is saying or feeling. You can acknowledge others' feelings but still disagree with their view of the situation. Firing employees usually involves exactly that. You can say, "I understand how hard this is on you and that you disagree with the company's decision," yet, at the same time, you can point out that they had received previous warnings and that termination should not be a surprise. This approach works in other negotiations as well because you must acknowledge that you understand why others are taking a position before you can begin to convince them to change it. When you say something like, "I understand why you are making that proposal," you are acknowledging that their position has validity. Often, that will allow them to recognize your needs and perhaps modify their own position in light of them. That opens the door to your following up the acknowledgment with an alternative proposal, such as, "Would the following idea also work for you…?"

Be Sincere

The most important part of being an effective listener is to genuinely care about what others are saying—to try to understand how they see things. Genuineness will make you a better listener and a more successful negotiator. People can usually tell if you are insincere. They know when you don't really care about what they think. Women who care about developing relationships have an advantage over men, who are just going through the motions of appearing to try to understand so they can get what they want. However, as mentioned earlier, just because you are genuinely trying to understand what someone else needs doesn't mean that you have to give up what you want. Even when, and perhaps especially when, you are collaborating, you need to remain focused on your own interests.

Listen "Under"

Pay attention not just to the words being spoken but to everything else that is going on as well. When you listen, you must hear not only the words but also discern what is really on the other person's mind. Watch the other person's body language, and pay attention to the feedback you are receiving. If, for example, as soon as you address one point of concern other objections are immediately raised, the stated objections are probably being used to mask the real issue which they may feel uncomfortable discussing. Any time someone takes a position that seems inconsistent with other information being conveyed to you, or if something just doesn't seem "right," delve deeper. Similarly, if someone appears to be agreeing with you, but you observe negative body language, continue to ask questions. Examples of unreceptive body language that you may observe include moving away from you, leaning back, crossing arms or legs, clenching fists, putting hands in pockets or behind the back, or turning away from you. Body language that suggests doubts includes touching the nose, rubbing the ears, running fingers through the hair, and looking sideways at, or turning the body sideways from, you. Whenever you see indications that what others are saying may not really reflect what they are feeling, draw upon your "listening under" skills. You can then call on the purposeful questioning skills discussed below to figure out what is really going on.

Ellen Sandles is Executive Director of the Tri-State Private Investors Network, an organization that brings together investors and new business ventures. Recently, she received a phone call from an investor who had been a guest at one of their meetings. He had attempted to call her several times before finally reaching her. She was hoping he would become a member, but he told her that, although the meeting had been excellent, he was not going to join. Ellen realized that what he was saying did not jibe with his behavior because people seldom go out of their way to call you to tell you "no." They wait for you to call them. So Ellen kept him talking until he told her what the real problem was. He wanted to take an active role in his investments, and in the past had served as CFO for a few of them. He was afraid that her group would view this as a conflict of interest. When Ellen assured him that they would not, he readily agreed to join. Initially, though, he hadn't expressed his real concerns. Ellen had to hear beyond what he was saying to understand that his need to tell her no didn't really mean "no." Rather, it meant that he wanted to talk about his concerns. Once she realized that, she could address them and persuade him to become a member.

Kitty D'Alessio, the first woman and first American to serve as President of Chanel, calls this skill "listening under." Developing the ability to listen under has helped her throughout her career. When she was a young advertising executive, she had a meeting with Charles Revson, then Chairman of Revlon, about shooting an ad for a new lipstick called "Naked Pink." Mr. Revson was a brilliant man with a big ego. He told her exactly how he saw the ad: "a wedding with the mother of the bride in a pink dress and wearing the lipstick." Yet he kept talking to Kitty about the sensuousness of the lipstick. She realized that this was the feel that he wanted for the ad, so she shot two versions: one the way he had described it to her, and the other with a more sensuous feel and using model Suzy Parker, wearing a big pink hat and pink bracelet—and nude from the waist up with her arms crossed in front of her breasts. She presented "mother of the bride" first, as her idea. He hated it, as she knew he would, even though it was exactly what he had described to her. But Revson loved the second concept and told her, "It was exactly what I wanted."

Had Kitty tried to talk him out of his "mother of the bride" idea initially, he wouldn't have listened and she might have even lost the account. Instead, she heard what he was really saying and allowed him to take credit for the idea. The way to get what she wanted, and "the point of this negotiation," according to Kitty, "was to 'lose' and let him think the Suzy Parker ad was what he had wanted all along." The "Naked Pink" campaign was a huge success, and it helped propel her career forward.

Make People Comfortable

One of the first things you should do when you negotiate is to make your counterparts feel comfortable with you. Before she begins settlement discussions, employment lawyer Nancy Erika Smith makes sure the room is at the right temperature, puts out food and coffee, and thanks everyone for coming. She wants people to feel comfortable so they feel free to open up.

What makes people feel comfortable differs from person to person. Feelings of comfort are often subtle and occur not only on the conscious but the subconscious level as well. The little things you do are important. Do your homework to find out what you need to do to make someone comfortable. For example, you might phone the other person's assistant and ask what the boss likes to drink so you can have it there. If food will be served, find out about likes and, equally important, dislikes. Make the people you are negotiating with feel like they belong.

ACTIVE LISTENING

There are numerous ways to encourage others to talk so you can find out what their real concerns are. These techniques are referred to as *active listening* and include the following:

Reflect Back

Restate what the other person has said in your own words. This ensures that you correctly understand what has been said, and it also shows the other person that you are trying to see things from their perspective. For example, if someone says, "I can't understand how you could come up with such an unworkable solution to our problem," you might paraphrase that by stating, "I guess we don't understand what your real needs are here."

Clarify

When something is not clear or you want a better understanding of what has been said, you can ask for clarification. For example, in response to the previous statement, you might say, "I don't understand. What do you mean by unworkable?" Or you could ask them to explain: "Why do you think it's unworkable?" In addition to giving you additional information, clarifying signals that you care about their concerns.

Encourage

Nod and smile, lean forward when others are talking, look them in the eye, and occasionally interject phrases such as "I see," "Go on," or "Really." This will encourage those who are speaking to expand upon what they are saying. The more they speak, the more information you will get. Again, by engaging in this behavior, you signal your willingness to listen and your interest in what is being said.

Acknowledge Effort

Provide positive reinforcement when the speaker tries to work with you or says something you agree with. For example, you might respond by saying "I appreciate your efforts," or "That's a good point." This will encourage further efforts to find common ground with you.

Recognize Feelings

It often helps to address the feelings that people may be experiencing but not openly sharing. In response to the statement that "The proposal is unworkable," you could reply, "I see that you're frustrated with how the discussions are proceeding." Recognizing others' feelings often defuses anger and allows them to open up. This is frequently necessary before you can move on to problem solving.

Summarize

When you believe that you understand the other person's point of view, summarize your understanding of what has been said and ask whether your understanding is correct. Do the same when you reach an agreement on a particular issue. Summarizing helps to prevent misunderstandings, and you should use it continually throughout the course of negotiations. When done on an ongoing basis, it reinforces that the parties are making progress and encourages continued efforts toward reaching an agreement.

It doesn't do much good to listen, however, if you don't act on what you hear. Don't be afraid to stray from what you had planned to say if you get signals that the other side is not receptive to the approach you are taking. Moreover, nothing works better than using what the other side says. You can achieve many of your objectives just by listening carefully to what is being said and agreeing to those points that are helpful. That is why it is always best to listen first.

PURPOSEFUL QUESTIONING

Good negotiators ask different types of questions for different reasons, from open-ended, information-gathering questions to focused questions intended to lead someone to a specific conclusion. The two primary reasons for asking questions during negotiations are to get information or to support your argument. How you ask a question will depend on what you are trying to achieve.

Ask Open-Ended Questions

You should ask open-ended questions if your goal is to obtain information or to find out what the other person is thinking. Open-ended questions can't be answered with a yes or a no. They usually begin with "who," "what," "where," "when," "why" or "how," which allow for wide latitude as to responses. Their unstructured nature often enables you to find out what the real issues are and how you might satisfactorily resolve them. Open-ended questions such as "Tell me how you reached that conclusion" can also give you an insight into how someone else thinks.

Often, asking the right question at the right time can give you the information you need to completely turn around a negotiation. I recall one such situation, which I described in my previous book. I was practicing law, representing an executive who was taking a job with a new company and being asked to relocate from California to Connecticut. We had worked out the major issues—salary, bonus, stock options—to his satisfaction. The new company had a generous relocation policy, but it provided for only a 30-day temporary living allowance. My client's daughter was a senior in high school and he was not going to move his family until after she graduated. So he asked the company to pay his temporary living expenses for one year. The company representatives insisted that they could not deviate from their relocation policy. My client was equally adamant and felt that if the company was taking such a bureaucratic approach to his request, it was probably not a place where he would want to work. Just when I thought the deal was about to fall through, I asked a question that allowed us to successfully conclude the negotiation. What was this brilliantly insightful question? It was simply "Why?" More specifically, I told the vice president of human resources that I couldn't understand why we were arguing about this issue. He explained that the relocation policy was written that way because the company had been burned by a senior executive who, after being paid temporary living expenses for well over a year, could not get his wife to move and rejoined his previous company. Having been embarrassed once, the vice president was not about to ask for another exception to the policy. Understanding his reasons for refusing our seemingly reasonable request enabled us to readily resolve the problem. We agreed that if my client did not move his family to Connecticut, he would repay the company for his temporary living expenses. This allowed the vice president to ask for and receive a modification to the relocation policy without the fear of looking foolish if things didn't work out.

Use Silence

After someone answers a question, you can use silence to elicit additional information. Just as nature abhors a vacuum, most people are uncomfortable with silence. If no one is speaking, there is a tendency to want to speak to fill the void. Therefore, simply remaining silent after others complete their answer will often cause them to continue speaking. Try this with your spouse, significant other, or friends. Ask a general question. Then, after they answer, just remain silent and continue to look right at them. Even if they appear to have finished, after a brief pause, they will almost always continue with their answer.

Adopt the Columbo Technique

Acting as if you don't understand something is also a way of getting information. If you ask lots of questions and seem to need assistance, others feel a natural inclination to help. This is sometimes referred to as the *Columbo* technique, after the TV detective played by Peter Falk who, by acting as if he did not understand anything, was always able to get the criminal to give him the information needed to crack the case. When you appear to be seeking help, others' defenses will drop, and they may unintentionally provide you with information that helps you make your case. For example, let's say you're looking to buy an antique table that's been advertised for $10,000. You meet with the owner and offer her $5,000. When she declines your offer, you say, "Even though I probably can't afford it, just so I know for the future, what would be a good price for a table like that?" You are now in a different position—no longer a serious buyer, but a neophyte collector seeking to tap her expertise. Although she might reply "$10,000," you are equally likely to get a more helpful response along the lines of, "You might get one for $8500 if you're lucky." Whereupon you can ask, "If I can get that much cash together, would you consider selling it to me?" Be careful how and when you use this technique, though. Never overuse it. Limit this approach to people who would be expected to be more knowledgeable than you. Otherwise it will undermine your credibility because people will begin to see what you are doing as disingenuous.

One purpose of asking open-ended questions is to keep the other side talking. The more someone talks, the more likely they are to provide valuable information. An added benefit is that it helps you develop a relationship with that person, which, in and of itself, is helpful. When you ask questions of others, people feel that you are working with them to find solutions, not negotiating against them.

Ask "Why?"

As mentioned above, often the most useful question you can ask is "Why?" Asking why works particularly well as a response to statements such as, "We can't agree to that" or "That would be contrary to policy." When you ask, "Why can't you agree to that?" or "Why do you have that policy?", you are calling for a reasoned response. After you are given a reason, you can make a case that the reason is not applicable in this instance. Alternatively, you have an opportunity to satisfy the other side's objections.

Repeat Back in Question Form

Another way to ask why is to use a variation on the reflecting back technique described above. Simply repeat what has just been said, but in question form. For example, if you are negotiating with a distributor with a New York–based sales force to distribute your product in the Northeast and the distributor wants exclusive rights to sell your product throughout the United States, you might use this technique as follows:

DISTRIBUTOR: We want an exclusive right to sell the product throughout the United States.

YOU: But you have no sales network outside the Northeast.

DISTRIBUTOR: We figure we'll be able to build one over the next few years.

YOU: You figure you'll be able to build one over the next few years?

Simply reflecting back the other side's own words when a proposal is not reasonable can be very effective. Similarly, when people make unqualified statements such as. "We never do that," a simple "Never?" will force them to either confirm that this is really the case, or, more likely, cause them to retreat to something like, "Except in very unusual circumstances." Once you get that kind of admission, you are well on your way to making your case because now you know what argument to make: that yours are unusual circumstances and require an exception to the normal practice. Once someone concedes that exceptions have been made in the past, it becomes much harder to claim that you don't deserve the same treatment.

Answer Questions with Questions

Sometimes you can answer a question with a question. If you don't want to respond to a particular question or you want to understand why someone is asking a particular question, you can respond by asking, "Well, what do you think?" If you do this too often you may appear evasive and argumentative, but using this approach sparingly can be effective.

Ask What They Would Do

Finally, if you find yourself at an impasse, you can always ask what they would do if they were in your position. This can sometimes completely change the dynamics of the negotiations by forcing the other side to come up with a solution to the problem, rather than trying to convince you that there is no problem. In doing so, a solution may emerge that would be acceptable to you or could be made so with slight modification.

Use Questions to Persuade

Author and former CNN executive Gail Evans recommends using questions as a way of making your argument:

> It's like negotiating with a two-year-old. No one can be more positional than a two-year-old. But you can negotiate around their technique. You never ask a question that can be answered with a no. If you can do that with a two-year-old, you can do it with a 10-year-old.

Golf course executive Cathy Harbin frequently uses questions to make a point when she is negotiating with men who want to hold tournaments at the top-ranked courses she manages. For example, if someone comes and blusters, "I want to have a tournament and pay $50 per person in greens fees. I want to bring donated beverages, and I also want a 20 percent discount on food and merchandise," she will repeat what they just said to her: "You want to pay $50 per person in greens fees, to bring donated beverages, and you also want a 20 percent discount on food and merchandise." Then she will ask, "Do you really think that is fair?" and wait silently for a response. That normally results in the prospective customer telling her what he really wants. For example, he might reply, "Well, what I really need is a $50 greens fee." Once she has that information, it's relatively easy to work out a deal acceptable to everyone.

Cathy also uses questions to make a point when a good golfer, usually a man who has never run a tournament, comes in to negotiate on behalf of his company or a charitable organization. Because he has played in a few tournaments, he may think he knows all about them. He may even believe he knows more about running tournaments than Cathy could because she is a woman. Cathy could tell him, when he asks for a $35 greens fee, that "he doesn't have a clue." She is sometimes tempted to do just that, but, if she did, she probably wouldn't get his business. So she subtly educates him by asking questions. The conversation might go something like this:

GOLFER: At the last tournament I played in they charged a $35 greens fee.

CATHY: Where was it held?

GOLFER: At Joe's Fleabag Motel and Golf Emporium.

CATHY: Is that a lot like our courses?

GOLFER: Not exactly.

CATHY: I see. Well, have you run tournaments before?

GOLFER: Not really, but my club runs one, and I was on the committee last year.

CATHY: OK, what type of format do you want to use?

GOLFER: I don't know. What would you suggest?

CATHY: Well, if most of the golfers are not in your league, maybe you should go with a scramble-and-play-best-ball. What types of contests do you want to have?

GOLFER: I hadn't thought about that. How about closest to the pin? How many should we have? What do you suggest?

CATHY: Maybe you might also want a longest drive contest? Do you want the beverage cart charged to the master account, or do you want the golfers to pay as they go?

GOLFER: I don't know. What do other companies do?

Soon the golfer realizes that he doesn't know as much about running tournaments as he thought. At the same time, Cathy makes it clear to him that her goal is to help make sure the event is a huge success. By the time they get down to negotiating price and the other details, their relationship has become more a collaboration about designing a great event while staying within the organization's budget than a negotiation about price.

ANCHORING

When developing a proposal, bear in mind that you can affect how people value things by the way you present them. We value what others value and we value things that are hard to get. Keeping this psychological phenomenon in mind will not only help you develop your initial proposal but also will help you understand when and how to offer concessions. People typically determine value by looking for a starting point, called an *anchor point,* and then making adjustments from there. Anchoring takes place when employers decide what salaries to offer job candidates. Ordinarily they use the candidate's current earnings as an anchor. If a job doesn't constitute a promotion and doesn't require relocation, a company will typically offer a 10 to 15 percent increase over someone's current salary. Even if a prospective employer recognizes that a candidate is being grossly underpaid, they will still use current salary as an anchor and make adjustments from that starting point. For example, if a candidate's current salary is really low, an offer might be increased to, say, 20 percent above that salary although that will still be much less than the market rate for the position. If employers do not know what candidates are currently earning, they usually look to the market rate to determine what to offer. That is why, in *Get More Money on Your Next Job,* I advise readers to avoid revealing their current salaries to prospective employers. Without current salary as an anchor, employers must rely on the market value of the position in formulating an offer. Understanding this phenomenon is particularly important for women, who often earn less than the market rate.

How well you negotiate often depends on what you choose as an anchor. As discussed in Chapter 10, if you allow a car salesperson to negotiate the purchase of a new car using the sticker price as the anchor, you will end up with a very different result than if you start with an offer based on the cost of the car to the dealer, information readily available on the Internet.

If the value of an item cannot be easily determined, anchors play a significant role in how we value it. When you go to a flea market or an antique shop, the price the seller places on an object serves as the anchor point and affects what you think the item is worth. Normally, the higher sellers set initial prices, the more they will end up getting for items. This leads to a basic rule of negotiating: Always ask for more than you expect to get. The higher you start, the more you will get. There is one basic exception to that rule: Pricing something clearly beyond what any reasonable person would pay for it can inhibit any further negotiations.

Set a Reasonable Anchor

To be accepted, anchors must be reasonable. Consider how you would react if you put your house on the market for $250,000 (a price you thought was reasonable, if perhaps a bit high), and someone offered you $100,000. You would dismiss the offer as ridiculous, reject it out of hand, and not even bother making a counter-offer. If you were offered $240,000, though, you would probably enter into negotiations with the prospective buyer. Interestingly, if you set your price at $255,000—still within a range that would be considered reasonable—you would probably end up selling the house for more. The same basic principle applies to counter-offers. So, if instead of the buyer offering $240,000, they offer $237,500, they will probably end up paying less for the house. So it is always in your interest to anchor your offer or your response, at the upper end for the seller or at the lower end for the buyer, of what would be considered reasonable.

How do you determine the range of reasonable possible outcomes normally referred to as the negotiating range? That depends on the nature of the negotiation. We talk about how to determine the negotiating range in specific situations in later chapters, which deal with buying a car, negotiating your salary, buying or selling a home, and negotiating a divorce. In general, you determine the reasonable negotiating range by looking at what others have agreed to in similar circumstances. What have comparable houses in the area sold for recently? What have women been awarded in alimony in similar situations? What pay do workers with equivalent skill and experience receive? How much do comparably equipped cars sell for? Answering these questions will give you the reasonable negotiating range. The Internet offers a wealth of information that can help you determine reasonable negotiating ranges in terms of salaries, home prices, and car costs. You can also get data from knowledgeable people in the relevant field—real estate brokers, divorce lawyers, and corporate recruiters. People you know who have recently engaged in similar transactions can provide useful information as well.

Remember, you get to choose the anchor that works to your best advantage as long as you can justify your choice. For example, in

Chapter 10 we suggest that you anchor your offer to purchase a car to the dealer's cost plus a small profit. Similarly, in setting your anchor when buying in a weak housing market, you might take the lowest price paid for a comparable house in the area and lower it by a certain percentage to reflect the softening market.

If you are faced with someone who anchors an offer too high, you should refuse to accept their anchor. If you respond to an anchor that is too high by giving a reasonable counter-offer, you will eventually find that you are either paying too much or that you cannot arrive at an agreement. These outcomes are rooted in how we normally negotiate and in our general concepts of fairness. When we negotiate, we tend to resolve issues by "splitting the difference." Therefore if one person anchors the negotiation too high, even though we recognize that fact, we still end up offering at some point to split the difference. Perhaps that split will not be 50/50 but if the other side starts very high they can concede more and still end up better off than if they started off with a reasonable offer and ultimately split the difference evenly.

As an example, suppose you respond to the offer of $100,000 for your house by countering with a reasonable counter-offer of $240,000, which is at the bottom of the range of reasonable values for the house. If the buyer now comes back with an offer of $225,000 for the house, your conversation might proceed as follows:

YOU: I won't go below $240,000.

BUYER: Tell you what I'm going to do. I'll offer you $230,000, but that is it.

YOU: The house is worth $240,000.

BUYER: Look, I've made huge concessions to you. We're not that far apart. Why don't we just split the difference?

YOU: $240,000 is a fair price.

SELLER: You're being unreasonable. I'm willing to move. Meet me halfway.

Eventually, you either give in and sell the house for less than $240,000 because you rationalize that it is not that big a difference, or you don't make the sale. Even if you don't agree to an even split, you will still sell the house for less than you could have gotten if you had refused to accept the initial offer. That is the best response to an unreasonable offer.

Insist that you get a fair offer to begin with, or refuse to consider it. There are many ways you can do this and still keep the door open for the other person to come back with a reasonable offer. You can say, "Could you tell me how you came up with that offer." If the other party cannot give you a satisfactory reason, you can say, "Perhaps you might want to go back and rethink your offer" or you could simply say, "I'd be happy to consider a reasonable offer if you come back with one, but I can't even consider what you're offering." If the other side asks what you are looking for, you can respond, "The asking price is very reasonable and that's what I'm looking for." Finally, you can use humor to make your point. For example, you might say, "If you think $100,000 is reasonable, perhaps I should counter with an offer of $350,000. That way we can both have a good laugh and then meet again when we're in a more serious mood." Whatever you do, though, you should not respond to an unreasonable offer by making a concession from your initial position.

As you can see, value is often as much psychological as it is real. The person who makes the first offer can play a critical role in determining what anchor the parties will use to view the rest of the negotiation. So, who should make the first offer? If you can determine the reasonable range of possible outcomes with a fair degree of certainty, then you should make the first offer. That way you can set the anchor. This is normally the situation when you are buying a car. As discussed in Chapter 10, if you have done your homework, you know approximately what the car is worth, what the dealer paid for it, and you are aware of any special promotions being offered to the dealer. That is why Kitty Van Bortel, the owner of one of the largest Subaru dealerships in the country, advises women to do their research and, then simply tell the salesperson what they are willing to pay.

If you are facing a situation such as an employment negotiation, in which the range of possible outcomes is less clear, try to get the other side to make the first offer. Otherwise, what you propose may be much less than what the other side would have offered had you allowed them to go first. On the other hand, you might ask for too much and price yourself out of consideration. This is a no-win situation for you. Unless you let the company make the first offer, you will end up asking for either too little or too much. There is one exception to this rule: If the person with whom you are negotiating is already looking at an anchor that is too low, you need to change the point of reference. For example, if your current salary is significantly below market and you have made the mistake of divulging exactly what you are earning, then you don't want the prospective employer to make the first offer. Rather, you must change the anchor. As discussed in Chapter 9, one solution is to provide information about the market rate for the position and make it clear that you expect to be paid at market. In that way, the market rate becomes the new anchor. Even better, get an offer from another company because that offer will become the new anchor and your current salary then becomes irrelevant.

Anchoring high is just as important when you are negotiating with your children as it is in business. Mothers know that instinctively. Donna Lagani, Cosmopolitan Group Publishing Director, describes how we do this with our children, beginning at a very early age. When discussing bedtime with her four-year-old, she sets her expectations high. If he says, "Mommy, can I stay up for another 15 minutes?", she will reply, "Another five minutes." If he says, "How about ten?", she will reply, "You are back to zero"—whereupon he will say, "I'll take five." Or, as Oxygen Media COO Lisa Hall puts it, "When her ten-year-old wants to stay up until ten o'clock and I am at nine, I know I will end up at nine-thirty." As your children get older, these discussions become more sophisticated, but the need to manage expectations by using appropriate anchors remains the same.

DELIVERING YOUR MESSAGE

If you have done a good job of listening and have asked the right questions, you will have laid the groundwork for delivering your message persuasively. Convincing is not just about the substance of your message, though; it is also about the messenger and how the message is presented. Put differently, your ability to persuade others to change the way they see things depends not only on what you say (content), but also on how you say it (tone) and on how you come across while you're saying it (body language). Although the content of your message is important, research has shown that how that message is delivered can be as important as the actual message itself.

Craft Your Message Carefully

Construct your message the way your ninth-grade English teacher taught you to write essays, with a theme, arguments in support of that theme, facts to buttress those arguments, and a structure for presenting them in a persuasive way.

Develop a Theme

After you marshal your facts, develop your proposal, and determine your best arguments, you must pull them together with a theme. Every negotiation should have a theme that serves as an organizing principle around which to structure the negotiations, and every element of your message should relate back to that theme. Tailor the theme to the people you are trying to persuade. You can do this in one of two ways. First, you can appeal to their self-interest. This is the type of appeal that usually comes to mind when we think of negotiations. Appeals of this type are based on what the other party wants or needs. It focuses on the other party's interests. For example, your appeal could be, "If you give me a raise, you will have my undying loyalty, hard work, and someone who can help you get the promotion you are hoping for." You could present the same arguments in the negative— "If you don't give me that raise, I'll leave, thereby depriving you of a loyal, hard-working employee whom you really need to get that promotion you want"—but arguments should generally be phrased positively. It is far more convincing to be for something than against something. This is why people who oppose abortion describe themselves as "pro-life" rather than as "anti-abortion."

The second type of theme appeals to values. Under certain circumstances, you may want to appeal to a sense of fairness or to focus on how your proposal benefits others (i.e., a charity). To appeal to others' values, you must understand what matters to them. That is why it is so important to find out everything you can about the people you are dealing with. Appeals to values can be particularly successful with family members or friends. Appealing to their generosity or desire to help will often have the desired impact.

When Lisa Caputo, now President of Citigroup's Women & Co., was Press Secretary to First Lady Hillary Rodham Clinton, she used just such an appeal to the values of the journalists covering the White House to convince them to respect Chelsea Clinton's privacy. In early 1993, for example, Mike Myers did a skit on *Saturday Night Live* making fun of Chelsea, who was 13 at the time. Lisa contacted NBC, but rather than trying to threaten or bully them, she appealed, as she later did with other journalists, to their human side. She appealed to them as parents: "Chelsea is just a kid. She did not run for office. She deserves as normal a childhood as possible under the circumstances. That's what you would want for your children, wouldn't you?" Although this issue arose periodically throughout the Clinton presidency, by and large, this appeal to values worked with the members of the press. As to the Mike Myers incident, he sent a letter apologizing, and NBC basically left Chelsea alone over the next eight years.

Themes are particularly important if you are dealing with people who represent organizations, whether the federal government or the local PTA, because you must not only satisfy the negotiator's agenda but also help them to sell the agreement to the members of the organization. My early experience as a labor negotiator taught me the importance of using themes. I learned to keep them simple and to make them ring true to my intended audience. For example, during one union negotiation when I was with Macy's during the 1980s, we chose the theme of "competitiveness." We argued that we needed to cut costs and become more efficient in the face of nonunion competitors. We highlighted the benefits of our becoming more competitive—the union would be able to preserve jobs and increase members' salaries. To buttress this theme, we pointed to all the unionized retailers who had gone out of business in the prior 10 years and we justified every proposal in terms of how it would make us more competitive. In the end, the union agreed, though reluctantly, to many of our proposals and was able to sell them to its membership.

The need to create a theme applies to personal situations as well. Former Macy's executive G. G. Michelson also started her career as a labor negotiator. At a time when there were very few female labor negotiators, she bargained with union leaders like Ron Carey, who later became President of the International Teamsters Union, and Peter Brennan, who later became Secretary of the U.S. Department of Labor. However, the negotiation she recounts most proudly was convincing her father to let her go to law school. She had just graduated from college and, in those days, very few women attended law school. Her father firmly believed that, although it was all right for G. G. to work, her goal should be marriage and a family. That being the case, her attending law school didn't make a lot of sense to him. So she developed a theme that was consistent with his view of marriage and family. She tried to persuade him that, since she had graduated from college at 19, she needed additional credentials to find meaningful work, even if only until she got married. She added that a law degree would help prepare her for a lifetime of useful work, even though it might be interrupted while she was raising a family. She succeeded in convincing her father because she never sought to challenge his core values or to change his views on marriage and family. Instead, she persuaded him that what she wanted was consistent with those values.

Consider the psychological needs of those with whom you are negotiating to determine what will motivate them to want to reach an agreement. Figure out what is preventing them from making a deal. Once you understand their motivation, you can develop a theme that meets those needs or overcomes those obstacles. When attorney Nancy Erica Smith is trying to settle an employment dispute, she always listens for the underlying "subtexts," unstated obstacles to settlement—and tries to determine what the other side needs to save face. Many times, she says, money is not the impediment. The parties are can usually figure out what a case is worth. Often, however, the person who initially made the decision being challenged, usually a termination, has a say in whether or not to settle. Even if this person is not directly involved in the settlement discussions, he or she may try to block a settlement because in their mind, settling equates to admitting to having done something wrong. When this situation arises, Nancy may try to develop a theme that places the blame on someone else. For example, she may fault someone else for withholding key information from the person who made the termination decision. This allows the decision maker to settle the case without having to admit doing anything wrong.

Highlight the Benefits to the Other Party and Repeat Them Frequently

Build your case around your chosen theme, which should highlight the benefits to the other party. Whether you are negotiating a million-dollar movie deal or deciding which movie to see with your husband, keep coming back to why your proposal will benefit the other side. Describe the benefits in different ways, and repeat your arguments to reinforce them. There is a saying in advertising: "Tell them what you are going to say. Say it. Then tell them what you just said."

Be Honest

People usually can tell if you are not being truthful. Your body language tends to give you away. Even if it doesn't, you may forget what lies you have told and eventually get tripped up. If you get caught in a lie while negotiating, you will lose all credibility. This does not mean that you're obligated to blurt out everything you are thinking and feeling. You can emphasize those points that support your position, you can phrase what you say carefully, and you can describe things in the light most favorable to your position—all these are part and parcel of the art of persuasion. But never lie. It's not only wrong; it's ineffective as well.

Structure Your Argument to Highlight Your Strongest Points

Once you decide on your message's content, you must decide on the most effective way to present it. Structure counts. Your message should have a powerful beginning and a strong ending. Generally, if the points you are making can grab the other side's attention, you should bring them up early in the process. That is why sales pitches often start out with interesting facts or statistics. For example, "Did you know that U.S. teenagers between 13 and 16 spend $3 billion annually on clothing?" If the important part of your argument is not particularly interesting or conveys information that the other party may resist or reject, you should build up to and end with it. Avoid burying important information in the middle of your message unless you hope to keep the other party from focusing on it. The same goes for your strategy in approaching various issues during a negotiation. Ordinarily, it is best to start with the easy issues and build up to the more difficult ones. That gives you a chance to develop a relationship and to see how the other side operates. At other times, however, you may want to talk through all the issues first before trying to resolve any of them. If time is an issue and you already have a relationship, you may want to try to solve the main issues first because the others will probably then fall quickly into line. Remember, your strongest points are those that demonstrate the benefits of what you are proposing to the other side.

Tailor Your Arguments to Your Intended Audience

Besides deciding on your most powerful arguments, you also want to consider which ones will play best to the people with whom you are negotiating. You want to present your argument in terms they will understand and relate to. One common mistake people make is to see things from what CEO Perspective Group Founder and Managing Partner Dee Soder, Ph.D., calls the "I perspective," in which, because you see something in a particular way, you expect someone else to see it the same way. For example, just because you are persuaded by logic does not mean that those with whom you are dealing will also be persuaded by logic. They may be more open to an emotional appeal.

Preparation can play a critical role in determining how you can best present your argument. CNN's Jan Hopkins describes one situation in which knowing her audience enabled her to gain the network's agreement to take on outside projects. She was scheduled to meet with the head of the network to discuss renewing her contract. Due to prevailing economic conditions, she felt that she had gotten about as much as she could in terms of salary, so she sought permission to work on outside projects that didn't interfere with her work at CNN. To find out how best to approach the topic with her boss, Jan spoke to his assistant, who suggested that, because the CEO was very bright and creative, it was usually best not to go in advocating a specific proposal. Rather, the assistant advised Jan to just bring up the problem, throw out some ideas, get him thinking about it, and then let him come back with a solution. That was how she handled the discussion, and it worked like a charm.

Lead, Don't Lecture

Jan's story illustrates a fundamental principle of persuasion: Whenever possible, try to lead other parties to the conclusion you want them to reach rather than just telling them. As discussed above, one way to do this is by asking questions. If the conclusion is complex, however, or the people with whom you are negotiating fail to get the point, you may have to lay out the conclusion for them. Similarly, if your intended audience starts out from a position antagonistic to yours, you may need to spell out in explicit terms why it's in their interest to agree to your proposal. If your argument is complex, try to break it down into its component parts. The simpler the argument, the more powerful it is. This is called the KISS formula—"Keep It Simple, Stupid." That is sound advice.

Anticipate Objections

It is also a good idea to anticipate the other side's objections by presenting both sides of the argument. That way, you can show why your position is the better one. Moreover, anticipating others' objections reduces the impact of their arguments when they finally make them. Another rhetorical device that is a very effective tool of persuasion is to "violate the other party's expectations." For instance, stating something that is not in your own self-interest and that you have not been forced to concede creates a very powerful effect. Not only does that point become more believable, but the rest of your argument gains credibility as well.

Use Experts to Support Your Positions

You may also choose to support your arguments by relying on experts or others whose opinions are respected by those with whom you are negotiating. Adding the weight of experts has tremendous psychological impact when you are negotiating and you can use them to great effect in your personal as well as your business dealings. For example, when Gina Doynow, manager in charge of College Credit Services for Citicorp, was decorating her apartment, she thought that a brown rug would go nicely in the living room. Her husband, however, had always hated brown. He would not even look at a brown rug. So she brought in their decorator, whose taste her husband respected. The decorator persuaded him to look at brown rugs, and today their living room features a beautiful brown rug—that her husband loves. Similarly, when G. G. Michelson was trying to convince her father to allow her to go to law school, she sought the help of two of her father's friends who were lawyers. They told her father that they thought she would make a great lawyer. Having the support of people her father respected had a psychological impact that far exceeded whatever specific point they made on her behalf.

A similar effect is achieved by presenting someone with a printed form or contract, or by citing a policy set forth in a policy manual. Like using an expert, basing your position on something "authoritative" provides the appearance of objectivity and makes it seem as if you are powerless to change your position. This tendency to defer to something "authoritative" is referred to as the "doctrine of legitimacy." When someone tells you, "That is the way it is always done," it is intended to do the same thing. While you may want to take advantage of this human tendency when negotiating with others, keep in mind that even if an expert says something or it is printed in a manual, you do not have to agree. You can always bring in your own expert, print up your own forms, or simply disagree. And, of course, you can respond to "This is the way it is always done" with "Well, we always do it this way."

Visual aids can also add legitimacy and authority to your position. Printed handouts, professional-looking slides, slick PowerPoint presentations, models, and other "props" will add credibility to your arguments. They also provide you with another psychological benefit: Most of the time, when people are listening to an argument, they are already thinking about their response rather than trying to understand what is really being said. Visual aids not only add legitimacy to an argument; they also force listeners to concentrate on what you are saying. Instead of thinking about their counter-arguments, your listeners will focus their attention on your visual aids in order to understand them. This will assist you in getting your points across.

Be Aware of How You Look When You Are Delivering Your Message

People who believe in what they are saying project an air of confidence. When you appear confident, others generally perceive you as more credible, and what you say is given more weight. We equate honesty and credibility with appearing relaxed, taking center stage, standing or sitting up straight, looking people in the eye, moving toward your audience, and projecting your voice. Although some people can appear totally confident even when they are not telling the truth and others come across as nervous and unsure of themselves even when they are being truthful, unconsciously people evaluate your credibility based on how you present yourself, as well as your arguments. So, as discussed earlier, be aware of your body language and the image you project.

TONE IS IMPORTANT

Just as important as what you say is how you say it. If you doubt that, think about the words to the children's lullaby, "Rock-a-bye Baby" ("Rock-a-bye baby on the tree top. When the wind blows the cradle will rock. When the bough breaks, the cradle will fall, and down will come baby, cradle and all.") The words are actually pretty gruesome, yet because of the soothing tone of the lullaby, we sing it to our children to calm them and put them to sleep. No one pays any attention to the words. As Marshall McLuhan said, "The medium is the message."

Tone is even more important when women negotiate. The generally accepted wisdom is that when you deliver a message, the tone should reinforce and be consistent with that message. However, when a woman is negotiating with a man, that may not be the best approach. As one senior executive we interviewed notes:

> As a woman, everything you say is magnified. It's easy to appear bitchy when you are taking a tough position. The thing that takes the edge off it is your tone. You can be strident if your position is easy, but a tough position should be delivered matter-of-factly. The tougher the message, the more you need to rein back the delivery, or you will overshoot the mark. Men are expected to match the tone to the position they are taking. Women should have them move in opposite directions.

Being firm in a quiet, soft-spoken manner is not only a very powerful way to present your message but also encourages others to be conciliatory. Moreover, when you are quiet but firm, you can use the principle of violating expectations to magnify the impact of what you say. As mentioned earlier, if you are normally low-key, on the rare occasions when you choose to raise your voice, even a little, you will have great impact— more than someone who constantly shouts or pounds on the table.

Even if you are soft-spoken, it helps to be passionate about your point of view. Lisa Caputo says that one thing she learned from watching Hillary Clinton was the importance of believing in what you are saying: "Your passion can persuade others. It is always an invaluable trait to be passionate about your beliefs and what you are striving for. Your passion makes your negotiating more credible and somewhat easier." Hearst Magazine President Cathleen Black puts it this way:

> If you are passionate about something, you can sell an idea. If you are passionate, it builds an inherent strength and confidence. All of us love to see real enthusiasm in the people around us. It is infectious. If you are enthusiastic, you will probably get more.

People can generally tell if you really believe in what you are saying. If you don't, you will find it very hard to convince anyone else to agree with you.

ADJUSTING YOUR MESSAGE AND USING CONCESSIONS

Even with all the preparation in the world, we can never fully predict how our message will be received. Negotiations by definition involve at least two parties. As soon as a second party is involved, you can no longer anticipate what will happen with any certainty. Your monologue becomes a dialogue. Military planners have a saying: "No plan survives contact with the enemy." That applies to negotiations as well. You must incorporate the other side into the process, constantly reframing your message to incorporate their input, and satisfying their expectations.

It is therefore important to manage expectations. If the other side's expectations are very high, no matter what you propose, it will not be enough. You can set expectations through your arguments and by properly anchoring the issues. *Cosmopolitan* Group Publishing Director Donna Lagani recommends that on key issues you set the expectations up-front. She calls this using "bulletproof statements." For example, at the beginning of negotiations with a potential new advertiser, she might say, "We will work with you, but there are certain things we won't do. We won't give away free advertising space to leverage additional business." Such statements take the issue off the table once and for all. If the subject comes up again, you can simply remind the person you are dealing with of what you said at the start of the negotiation.

You can also reduce expectations by not granting concessions too quickly. The harder it is to gain a concession, the more people value it. For example, a friend of mine just received a raise. It wasn't much. Ordinarily, she would have been insulted by such a paltry increase. But it was long past the time when raises had been given in previous years. Because her company was seeking to reorganize under the bankruptcy laws, she hadn't expected to get any raise at all and was therefore happy with what she received.

You must not only listen but also respond to what is said. You can respond in one of three ways: by addressing their arguments, by modifying your position to better satisfy their interests, or by granting concessions. When you negotiate, you'll normally do all three at one time or another.

Instead of focusing on where you disagree, start by emphasizing the points you have in common. Focus on the areas where the other side seems most receptive. Try to reach early agreements on issues to which they respond favorably so you can develop a level of trust and cooperation. Constantly reformulate your message to reflect their input. Use their words wherever possible, and give them credit for their ideas. Constantly adjust your message based on the feedback you are receiving. If you want to win them over, you must allow them to have significant input in the process. Because negotiating is a process that requires give and take, you must allow others sufficient time to feel that their views have been fully taken into account. Only after that occurs will it be possible to reach an agreement.

Making concessions before the other side is ready to respond in kind will only result in raising their expectations. How do you know how much time is necessary? It depends on the parties' relationship and on what is at stake. But a good rule of thumb is, the more important the subject is to the other side, the more time you should spend just talking about the issues before you make any concessions. If you discuss all the issues and listen carefully to what those on other side are saying before you make any concessions, you will have a better understanding of what is important to them.

As mentioned earlier, you are expected to make concessions when you negotiate. If you advertise an antique desk in the newspaper for $1000 and the next morning, first thing, someone comes by and offers to pay that, your immediate reaction will be that you priced it too low. On the other hand, if the buyer tries to get you to sell it for $950 even if the buyer *eventually* agrees to pay you $1000, you will feel that you got a fair price. Negotiating is a process that you can seldom short-circuit. It requires give and take. More often than not, others will expect you to be willing to modify your initial position, at least a little.

Cultural norms dictate that if one party makes a concession, the other should respond in kind. By making a concession, you encourage others to do the same. Each time the two of you make a concession, you move closer to an agreement. You can also use concessions when negotiations begin to bog down or when you cannot agree on a particular issue.

Be careful not to make concessions too quickly, even on matters that are not important to you. Because, as discussed above, people do not value what they get too easily, it is best not to make concessions too early or too readily. Just because you agree to something early on doesn't mean that the other side will respond in kind later, if the negotiations hit a rough spot. When it comes to concessions, people have short memories.

Also, always treat any concession you make as important. Otherwise, your gesture will not have its desired effect. If what you are offering is important to the other side, it ought to be important to you. Treat it that way. For example, rather than simply agree, you might say, "I don't know if I can do that; I'll have to check with my boss. If I can get her to agree, would you be willing to...?"

Concessions should not be used in such a way as to undermine your theme. But you can use concessions to show that you have heard what the other side has said. You can justify changing your position as an attempt to accommodate the other party's interests or on the basis of new information that the other side has given to you. It is also a good idea to vary your use of concessions. Sometimes you can simply concede on a given point and follow up with a request for something else. At other times, you might offer to trade one thing directly for another. And you may occasionally simply concede something to gain some goodwill.

Finally, always ask for more than you expect to get, and keep something in reserve to help persuade the other person to close the deal. As the process moves toward its conclusion, you can use concessions to maximum effect and thereby gain something that would have been impossible to obtain earlier. The longer the negotiations have gone on, the more everyone will want to ensure that an agreement is reached. Moreover, granting concessions toward the end of the negotiations effectively allows the other side to go away feeling good. The most effective negotiations are those in which you convince someone to do what you want, yet they walk away feeling that they have "won."

4

Collaborate

Changing to a Problem-Solving Approach, or How to Satisfy Everyone's Interests

Kitty D'Alessio had just been appointed President of Chanel. She was the first woman, and the first American, ever to hold that position. She inherited a chief designer who she didn't believe had the right feel for the line. She wanted to replace him and decided that Karl Lagerfeld would be perfect for the job. Although she didn't know him personally, she knew that he was involved in a number of different ventures and was making lots of money. In addition to designing clothing for Chloe, he was designing furs for Fendi and was selling fragrances under his own label, Parfum Lagerfeld. She arranged to get an introduction to Karl through Grace Mirabella, the Editor of *Vogue*. That night she flew out to meet him at his home in Italy.

The two hit it off instantly. After speaking for several hours she offered him a job. She said, "I don't know what I'll do if you say no—your name can't be on the label and I can't pay you a lot at first, but I want you to design couture and ready-to-wear for Chanel." He responded that he "would love to do it, but couldn't possibly give up everything else that he was doing." Sensing the moment, she instinctively responded: "Who is asking you to give up anything?" Ultimately, Kitty got the approval she needed and put together the deal. Karl accepted much less money than he could have gotten elsewhere but was allowed to continue with his other business ventures. The key to hiring Karl Lagerfeld, which most credit with rejuvenating the Chanel brand, was Kitty's ability to listen to him and understand his needs and desires. Having done that, she was able to figure out how to accommodate those needs and still satisfy Chanel's interests.

This is an example of *collaborate* at its best. As mentioned in Chapter 1, most women are more comfortable with a "relational" negotiating style than with the "competitive" style favored by men. Women also have several advantages over men when it comes to negotiating collaboratively. They tend to be able to read others and figure out what's important to them. They can often sense what is going on beneath the surface and are generally better than men at developing and maintaining the relationships that are key to negotiating collaboratively.

So long as women keep their own interests firmly in mind, those relational skills can help them negotiate effectively by finding ways to meet other's interests while also satisfying their own. Kitty Van Bortel, who built one of the largest Subaru dealerships in the country by catering to women, describes the essence of collaborating when she states that the "secret of my success is helping others get what they want."

Most books that deal with collaborative, or "win-win" negotiating start by discussing listening or identifying interests. While both of these are important, this picture will give you a better under-

standing of what collaborative negotiating is all about. We begin our discussion of collaboration by asking you to look at this picture.

What do you see in this drawing, which is based on one first published by W. E. Hill, in a 1915 issue of *Puck* Magazine? Do you see a beautiful young woman, or an old, ugly one? The problem is that once you look at the picture one way, it is difficult to see it the other way. Look carefully, and you will be able to. The old woman's prominent nose can also be a young woman's face in profile. Her thin-lipped smile becomes the beautiful young lady's choker. But you have to work at seeing the picture another way. Once your mind sees one it is difficult to visualize the other. No matter how hard you try, you cannot see both images at the same time. The same is true for collaborative negotiating. If you focus on one solution too early on, it becomes very difficult to recognize others that might better accommodate both sides' interests.

Collaborating is problem solving. It requires keeping everyone's interests in mind to come up with a solution that meets all their needs. Employment attorney Nancy Erica Smith describes this as "multitasking," which she believes women do better than men. In her words, when you collaborate: "You are not seeking to win, but to find common ground. You are trying to meet many people's needs. Good negotiators can take into account their goals and the needs of the other side." Often the solution lies not so much in being creative as in being exhaustive. If you consider all the possible options, it is likely that at least one, and possibly several, will satisfy everyone's interests. It is not uncommon, however, for negotiations to break down, even when both parties are committed to working together, because one side locks into a solution early in the process and is not open to consider other alternatives. That is why when you collaborate, the starting point is to list all of the possible options.

Avoid fixing on any one solution until you have thoroughly explored the advantages and disadvantages of all your options because the minute you identify a preferred solution, you become less open to other possibilities. You move almost instinctively into a convince mode rather than a collaborative one. To collaborate successfully, force yourself to remain flexible and open to other possible solutions,

In their seminal work *Getting to Yes: Negotiating Agreement Without Giving In,* the authors describe a method for engaging in negotiations called "principled negotiations." This is a form of collaborating that treats negotiations as problem solving. The goal is to find a good solution that is mutually acceptable. When properly used, it is an excellent method of negotiating. We are greatly indebted to the authors, and drew heavily upon their work in developing our ideas about collaborating.

There are times, however, when you will not be able to use this approach. *Collaborate* can succeed only if the other party genuinely wants to work with you. You can sometimes create a situation in which someone who is not initially inclined to collaborate chooses to do so. However, that is not always possible. *Collaborate* is based on trust. It requires that you either have or develop a relationship with your counterparts. The open and honest communications, which are essential to the process, can really occur only where a relationship exists. Otherwise, the temptation to gain an immediate advantage by manipulating the process outweighs the benefits of working toward a mutually beneficial solution. All the "negotiating jujitsu" in the world will never make a used car salesperson negotiate collaboratively with you. Nonetheless, understanding the salesperson's interests and negotiating in a way that satisfies those interests can be effective. Alternatively, as discussed in Chapter 10, you can simply *create* another way to buy a car that avoids the haggling which normally accompanies a visit to a used car dealer.

As we see it, *collaborate* entails four basic steps: developing a relationship, understanding the other parties' interests, identifying options, and agreeing on a mutually acceptable solution from among those options. Once you understand the other parties' interests and have explored all the possible solutions, you can determine which one best meets everyone's needs.

DEVELOP A RELATIONSHIP

When I teach my negotiating class, I use an exercise in which I ask my students to play the role of two adults who each want to buy the same bicycle for their daughters. The store has only one bicycle left in stock. One parent wants the bicycle for her daughter's birthday party the next afternoon; the other parent wants it so his daughter can use it in a race the following morning. Neither "parent" knows at the outset why the other wants the bicycle. There is an obvious collaborative solution: One parent gets to use the bicycle in the morning for the daughter's race. Then the bicycle is cleaned up and given to the other girl for her birthday. Students usually arrive at some variation of this solution if they openly share their reasons for wanting the bicycle.

When two women are paired, they invariably reach this solution. When a man and a woman are paired, they also usually reach this result. When two men are paired, they sometimes reach this solution, but often they don't, and, on rare occasions, they get so angry at each other that I have to intervene. When the parties cannot reach an agreement, I tell them to assume that, instead of being strangers who meet for the first time at the store, they are next-door neighbors. Invariably, within minutes they share their reasons for wanting the bicycle and reach the collaborative solution. This exercise illustrates not only how well collaborative negotiating can work in the right circumstances but also how important it is to develop enough of a relationship to find out why others want what they want. My female students do this instinctively, but I sometimes have to manufacture the relationship for my male students. Without that relationship, though, *collaborate* doesn't work. The parties' relationship encourages taking a long-term perspective and allows the honest and open communications essential to the process. By creating a relationship, you cause the other party to have a stake in reaching a mutually satisfactory outcome.

Relationships are the cornerstone to negotiating success. We all have lots of choices in life about whom we want to hire, whom we want as friends, and whom we want to do business with. We all prefer to deal with people we like. People will do business with you because they respect you and enjoy working with you. If they want to work with you, they will look for ways to make that happen rather than finding reasons why it can't. It's also harder for others to say no to you if they like you. You don't, however, have to sacrifice your own interests to maintain a relationship. If others try to use their relationship with you in that way, in all likelihood the relationship is not what you think it is.

Terrie Williams is President of the Terrie Williams Agency, a public relations firm that has represented, among others, actor Eddie Murphy, jazz musician Miles Davis, baseball Hall of Famer Dave Winfield, pop star Janet Jackson, and attorney Johnnie Cochran. For her the essence of negotiating lies in developing relationships with the people with whom she works:

> To the extent you can develop a rapport with the person you are negotiating with, you can get almost anything. Any rule can be bent, broken, or cease to exist if you have the right relationship.

Katie Ford, CEO of the Ford Modeling Agency, also works hard at developing and maintaining relationships with her models and with the clients who hire them. For example, Ford represents Patricia Velasquez. Katie has known her for 10 years. They have traveled together, done shows together, and even worked on charities together. Patricia is spending most of her time these days focusing on her acting career and has just completed work on a sequel to *The Mummy*. Notwithstanding, Ford has just gotten *Cover Girl* magazine to sign Patricia to an exclusive cosmetics contract promoting their products. Were it not for the relationship that Katie and Patricia have developed over the years, Ford might not have still been representing her and she might not have gotten the Cover Girl campaign.

Similarly, Jeanette Chang, International Publishing Director at Hearst Magazine International, credits her success to the relationships she has developed over the years. She puts that philosophy into practice on a daily basis. Almost all her business associates have become her friends over the years. To make the most of your relationships, it helps if you become a more interesting person, and she suggests doing that by developing an area of expertise outside your work. Hers, for example, is Asian art. The more interesting you are, the more people will want to spend time around you. That, in turn, makes it easier to develop relationships—and, as an added benefit, to negotiate.

DEVELOP THE RELATIONSHIP BEFORE YOU BEGIN NEGOTIATING

It is always better if you develop the relationship before you ever have to negotiate with someone. Although people may be suspicious if you attempt to do so immediately before you begin negotiating, if your efforts are sincere, they are still likely to succeed. So, even if you have not been able to develop a relationship ahead of time, try to do so at the start of the process. There are any number of ways you can do that, but they all require one thing: having a genuine interest in getting to know the other person.

Carole Cooper, one of the owners of the N.S. Bienstock Agency, is one of a handful of successful female agents who represents on-air talent in news and reality television. When Carole negotiates with someone she doesn't know, she begins by trying "to connect with the person she is with as a person." Her preparation includes finding out about people's interests, their ratings, industry gossip of interest to them, and other personal information. When she meets someone for the first time, she "talks about the pictures in their office, about their family, about the view" in an effort to get to know them.

Terrie Williams tries to do the same thing by getting together with people "in a relaxed atmosphere, for dinner or drinks, and tries to find out what they are all about." Her business partner calls this "opening a person's significance." If you can zero in on what matters most to others, you will better understand how to negotiate with them and how to appeal to them. The more you build relationships, the more successful your negotiations are likely to be.

><+>+O+<+><

Develop Trust Over Time

Because I grew up negotiating with my dad, I learned that, by developing a relationship based on trust, I was able to negotiate effectively, although I did not think about it in those terms at the time. When I was a teenager, my father refused to let me get a credit card. He didn't believe that high school students needed one. So I had to negotiate with him each time I wanted to borrow his to go shopping. He would never just hand it over; he always insisted that I have a good reason for needing it. Afterwards, however, I would avoid returning the card to him immediately. When he asked for it back, I usually managed to find a reason why it was a good idea for me to keep it for a few more days, but my real reason was to get him comfortable with the idea that I could be trusted not to use it without permission. Over time, it became commonplace for me to borrow it, even though he would always resist and argue with me. After a while, he accepted the idea that it was a good idea for me to have a credit card, or maybe he just got used to my having it. Eventually, he stopped asking me to give it back. Before that happened, though, I had to earn his trust.

To get what I wanted from my dad, I had to do it a little bit at a time. Sometime that is the only way to achieve your goals. In negotiating, this is sometimes referred to as the "bologna technique." You ask for the bologna one slice at a time until eventually you have the whole thing. If you had asked for the whole bologna at once, though, you never would have gotten it. That was the case so far as my getting a credit card was concerned.

When it was time for me to go to college, I pleaded my case one more time, only this time more directly. I told my dad that I might need a credit card for emergencies, for food, and for gas once I got a car. I promised that I would not abuse the privilege. If he ever felt that I was taking advantage, he could make me repay him. (Letting others know that you realize they have power over a situation when they actually do lends credibility to what you are saying.) By that time, I had developed a relationship with him based on trust. When I needed to, I was able to call upon that trust.

>—i—<>—O—<>—i—<

YOUR RELATIONSHIPS WITH OTHERS CAN FACILITATE NEGOTIATIONS

In developing a relationship with someone, it helps to have mutual friends or acquaintances. That is why, when you first meet someone, you usually mention people you think that person might know. This approach also works when you are trying to develop a relationship in the context of negotiating. Do you recall the story of how Kitty D'Alessio hired Karl Lagerfeld for Chanel? Before she called Karl, Kitty asked a mutual friend, Grace Mirabella, the Editor of *Vogue,* to call him. Kitty used that connection to create an instant relationship upon which she could draw when she met with him.

Letting those with whom you are negotiating know that you have mutual friends serves a second purpose as well. That knowledge encourages collaborative negotiations. Even if you know that you will never negotiate with this person again, you are less likely to engage in questionable conduct to gain a short-term advantage if you know that they will be talking about you with your mutual friends at some future date.

You can also use your relationships with people not directly involved in the negotiation to influence the process. Susan Medalie, Executive Director of the Women's Campaign Fund, considers her greatest asset as a negotiator to be her "talent for figuring out connections—who she knows that might be able to help." Often when you need something, your most important task may well be to figure out the right person to ask.

When Susan was Deputy Director of the U.S. Holocaust Council, she arranged a "Day of Remembrance Dinner" in the rotunda at the Smithsonian. This is a very elegant setting for an event and very difficult to get permission to use. One prominent feature in the rotunda is a huge pendulum that swings back and forth 24 hours a day, seven days a week. She became concerned that some of the guests might get motion sickness watching the pendulum while eating dinner. She also knew that it would be extremely difficult, if not impossible, to convince the Smithsonian administrators to stop the pendulum for any reason, let alone a fund-raising dinner. So she called Illinois Congressman Sidney Yates, a strong supporter of the Holocaust Council. Through his committee assignments in Congress, he had influence over the Smithsonian's appropriations. He was able to help her persuade the Smithsonian staff to stop the pendulum while dinner was being served. Sometimes the critical questions in any negotiation are "Who is going to ask whom, and how are they going to ask?" Relationships can play a key role in answering those questions.

Little things can make a big difference in developing relationships. Whenever Jeanette Chang goes to meet with someone, for instance a designer who might advertise in one of her magazines, she reads up on fashion trends in the designer's area, looks at local newspapers, and tries to find out as much as she can about the company and the designer personally. She always tries to bring them an appropriate gift, based on the personal knowledge she has gathered about whether they are married, divorced, have children, and so forth. As she says, "Relationships require work and I give them 150 percent." Jeanette feels her efforts have paid off and helped her to succeed in negotiating all aspects of her life.

TAKE THE LONG-TERM VIEW

Build relationships even when you see no immediate prospect of working together with someone. Sometimes people who might make excellent negotiating partners are not in a position to do business with you at that particular moment. Even though you are not currently working with someone engaged in a negotiation at that moment, you can still take advantage of the opportunities that arise to develop a relationship. Cosmopolitan Group Publishing Director Donna Lagani describes a situation in which she was trying to sell advertising to a cosmetics company. The firm had just installed a new management team and did not have any advertising money available. Nonetheless, she met with several of the executives. During that meeting they mentioned a problem they were having, attracting and keeping good beauty advisors to sell their lines in retail and department stores. Donna offered to hold a contest for their beauty advisors and to feature the winners in *Cosmopolitan*. Although the company was not purchasing any advertising at that moment, Donna was willing to help the company because she wanted to develop a relationship. As a result, she was able to stay in touch with the company's marketing people at a time when they were not meeting with any other magazines. Eventually, when the company began to advertise again, *Cosmopolitan* was in an excellent position to garner a large share of that advertising due to the established relationship with the company's marketing department.

Sometimes people are just not ready to enter into collaborative negotiations. Bonnie St. John, an amputee from the age of five who went on to be a silver medalist at the Para-Olympics, a Rhodes scholar, and a White House staff member, is an inspirational speaker and the author of *Succeeding Sane* and *Getting Ahead at Work Without Leaving Your Family Behind*. When she first became a professional speaker, she and one of the speakers bureaus she worked with began negotiating about the possibility of their having an exclusive relationship. By her own admission, she was not ready to enter into collaborative negotiations and went into the negotiations with a long list of demands, including a guarantee of at least 40 speaking engagements a year and a limited right to continue working with other bureaus. They, of course, declined to agree to her demands but said, "Why don't you just continue to work with us? If you like us, then we can work out an exclusive arrangement." She did, and a year later, because of the relationship they had developed and her own change in attitude, they entered into an exclusive deal. By then, she had stopped viewing an exclusive relationship as a loss of control that required her to protect herself and had come to view it as the creation of a team that would work together for everyone's mutual benefit. With that change in attitude, she was able to negotiate an agreement that resulted in her getting more than 40 speaking engagements in the first year, but in her fees going up and in her receiving other benefits that she would never even have thought to ask for.

IDENTIFY AND EXPLORE EACH PARTY'S INTERESTS

The key to collaborative negotiating is understanding the other party's interests. Most negotiating involves taking positions—trying to convince the other side that it is in their interest to accept what you are offering. If they don't agree, you can follow up by either modifying your arguments, granting additional concessions, or devising some combination of both, as was discussed in Chapter 3. Thus you start with your proposed solution, and your counterparts start with theirs. You each work on convincing the other to move towards your position by constantly readjusting your arguments and your proposal. In *Getting to Yes,* the authors refer to this as "positional bargaining." Instead of focusing on positions, they suggest that you focus on interests. "A position" refers to what you want; an "interest" is why you want it. The classroom exercise discussed earlier illustrates the difference. Each of the "parents" wants the bicycle. If they insist on positional bargaining, the negotiation will go something like this:

"FIRST PARENT": Excuse me, I'm buying that bike.

"SECOND PARENT": Sorry, I was here first.

"FIRST PARENT": Actually, I was here first and was talking to that salesman over there about buying the bike before you got here.

"SECOND PARENT": Well, I had called over here and asked them to hold it for me.

"FIRST PARENT": Well, obviously they didn't, since I don't see any hold sign on it.

"SECOND PARENT": Even though I was here first, to avoid a fight, how about if I give you $10 and I take the bike?

"FIRST PARENT": How about if *I* give *you* $10 and *I* take the bike?

The first parent's interest is in giving the bicycle to her daughter at her birthday party the next afternoon; the second parent's interest is in having the bicycle so his daughter can use it for a race the next morning. Without knowing each other's underlying interests, the parties cannot reach an agreement. Yet by discussing their respective interests, they can readily achieve a mutually beneficial solution.

There are many different types of interests. There are substantive interests, such as how much money something will cost or how quickly it can be obtained. There are interests in the process by which an agreement is reached, which can touch on questions such as, "Was it fair?" "Was I allowed to fully participate?" "Was I treated with respect?" Different parties can have different types of interests. One may care deeply about certain specific substantive issues, while another may consider the parties' relationship more important. Sometimes people can have competing interests. If you understand that, you may be able to achieve your goal despite initial resistance. For example, Emily Menlo Marks, Executive

Director of United Neighborhood Houses of New York, was seeking support for an ad against police brutality at a time when the police were engaging in an aggressive stop-and-frisk program. She met with the Human Resources Council, a group that consists of a number of charitable organizations, and argued that they needed to do something about the problem. The head of the council argued against the ad on the grounds that such a stand would mean coming out against the mayor and perhaps jeopardizing future funding for the member organizations. In response, Emily stood up and said, "If we don't take a stand on this, who will?" As a result, by appealing to the council members' sense of what was right, Emily was able to get a number of members to sign on to the ad even though it might not have been in their political interest to come out against the mayor.

LOOK FOR DIFFERENCES IN HOW THE PARTIES VALUE THINGS

Different people also value things differently. When you are attempting to explore options, you can often find collaborative solutions by taking those differences into account. Consider how two business partners might agree to split up the profits from their business. One partner might need money today to buy a vacation home, while the other might be more interested in income 10 years from now when she plans to retire. They could agree to allow the one partner to take money out of the business now in return for the other partner getting a larger percentage of the profits as they increase over time. In another situation, one party might be willing to take certain risks, whereas another might be uncomfortable taking any risk at all. This could result in one partner getting a greater share of the profits in return for guaranteeing the other partner a minimum annual return. Or, if one partner believes that the business has peaked while the other thinks it will continue to become more profitable over time, they might agree that the first partner will receive a greater share of the profits for the next few years in return for accepting a smaller portion five years hence.

Good negotiators take advantage of differences in the way people value things and the relative importance they place on various issues. Patricia Hambrecht is President of Harry Winston, a jewelry company that deals in some of the rarest and most beautiful jewelry in the world. Her efforts to hire top model Carolyn Murphy provides a good illustration of how to take advantage of different interests. Carolyn had offers to work for several competing jewelers but wanted to work with Harry Winston because of the quality of the merchandise. Patty didn't have the advertising budget to pay her what she could command elsewhere, so she offered to pay Carolyn partly in cash and partly with jewelry. That way Harry Winston could afford her services, and she got the jewelry she loved. Moreover, the cost of the jewelry to the company was less than the value Carolyn placed on it or what she would have had to pay if she could have found comparable pieces elsewhere.

Even interests that might seem insignificant to you may be important to the person you are dealing with. Carole Cooper described one negotiation she had with the manager of a local television station in the Midwest on behalf of an anchor/reporter that she represented. Carole wanted to significantly increase her client's salary. The station manager recognized her client's talent but had problems with some of her work habits. He told Carole, "I know you want more money, but I have some problems with her. She spends a lot of time making personal phone calls." Instead of arguing with him about whether the client did or did not make too many calls or whether, even if she did, it affected her ability to do her job, Carole replied, "I run an office. I understand. I'll talk to her." She did, and, when she and the station manager spoke again a few weeks later, he couldn't thank her enough because, after talking with Carole, her client ceased making personal calls from the office. That resolved, they were in short order able to agree on a new contract with a significant salary increase for her client. To Carole, "It was a little thing, but it helped a lot."

The difference between getting what you want and losing the deal can depend on how well you understand the other party's interests. Developing a relationship with them will allow you to better understand what they value. If you do it well, you can use that information to creatively reach an agreement. Hollywood producer, director, and writer Tamar Simon Hoffs was able to convince a wealthy businessman to invest in a movie she was producing when she found out that his son was interested in getting into filmmaking. She obviously had to convince him that the deal made sense financially, but she clinched the deal by offering to give the investor's son his first movie job. That was more valuable to the investor than the profit he would eventually make from the film.

DETERMINE WHY THE OTHER SIDE IS TAKING PARTICULAR POSITIONS

To identify interests, try to put yourself in the other parties' shoes. See if you can argue their position. Ask yourself "Why?" and "Why not?": Why is someone taking a particular position? What interests are being served? What are the obstacles to reaching agreement? Why hasn't your adversary already agreed to what you are proposing? A person may have several different interests in any given negotiation. Moreover, various people on the same side may also have different interests. You must satisfy not only the people with whom you are dealing directly but also the people who are not at the bargaining table but who have influence over the process. For instance, the person across the table may have a boss currently under consideration for a promotion. If that is the case, the boss is likely to care more about the immediate impact of any agreement than about what will happen five years hence, and you need to bear that in mind when you negotiate.

GENERATE OPTIONS

We started this chapter by talking about how focusing too quickly on a desired outcome can inhibit collaboration. An essential element of collaborative negotiating is to come up with an exhaustive list of possible solutions. You can then identify all those that satisfy the interests of all parties and choose from among them. Generating such a list should be part of your preparation. It will be useful no matter how you approach the negotiations. If, during the negotiations, you feel the parties have developed a relationship that allows for collaboration, you can revisit the list as a joint effort. For the reasons discussed earlier, the purpose of this exercise is to develop a comprehensive list of options that you can draw upon as the negotiations proceed; it is not to evaluate them.

You can employ a variety of approaches to develop possible solutions. Let's take as an example a husband and wife who are trying to decide where to take their annual vacation. They are on a limited budget and can afford to take only one vacation. She would like to go to Italy because she loves fine dining and wants to go sightseeing and shopping. He wants to go to the Bahamas to gamble and lie on the beach.

Trade

One possible solution would be to go to Italy this year and to the Bahamas next year. Or, if there is more than one interest involved, as if often the case, trade one off against the other. For example, if she prefers to take their vacation during the summer and he wants to take it in the winter, they could agree that one would get to choose the time and the other could choose the place.

Expand the Pie

Another possible option is to readjust their lifestyle so they can afford two vacations. Perhaps he could write his novel in the evening and take a job as a reporter with a local newspaper to earn extra income. Because she likes to garden, perhaps she could agree to take care of the lawn and garden herself instead of paying a lawn service.

Couple Interests

A third approach is to identify other interests and introduce them into the negotiation. Adding something new to the mix creates the opportunity to satisfy another interest of one of the parties rather than fight over how to divide up the resources being discussed. For instance, the couple could agree that if she goes to the Bahamas, he'll spend Christmas at her mother's.

Identify Different Ways to Satisfy Everyone's Interests

By looking beyond each party's stated positions to their underlying interests, you can sometimes identify solutions that neither has previously considered but that satisfy everyone's interests. Taking into account each party's underlying interests—golf and the beach for him; exotic cuisine, shopping, and sightseeing for her—might result in their finding a vacation destination that allows them each to do what they want. Perhaps Hawaii would work for both of them.

AGREE ON A MUTUALLY ACCEPTABLE OPTION

After you list all the available options, you still have to agree on one. Based on the above examples, you would think that, if you are just creative enough and come up with enough options, an obvious "best" solution will emerge. That sometimes occurs.

More often than not, though, even after all the options have been identified, the parties still need to negotiate about which one to choose.

We believe that there is no single right way to reach an agreement. What works best depends on the type of problem, the relationship between the parties, and the nature of their interests. If you want to collaborate but the other person doesn't, and their interests are diametrically opposed to yours, relying solely on a collaborative approach will probably fail. You may have to first *convince* the person to see things differently or *create* a totally different approach to dealing with the issue. In fact, in most negotiations you will want to draw on all three of the major concepts we present in the book: *convince, collaborate,* and *create.*

Harry Winston President Patricia Hambrecht experienced how all three concepts can come into play when, while still President of Christie's North America, she negotiated for the right to handle the sale of Vincent van Gogh's *Portrait of Dr. Gachet.* The lawyer for the family that owned the painting made a number of demands, but one of the major issues was that the family have the absolute right to withdraw the painting from auction if there was a major decline in the stock market. He believed that if the markets declined significantly, it would affect the price that the painting would fetch. Because Christie's would be spending almost a million dollars to promote the auction, Patty could not agree to allow the painting to be withdrawn except under the most extreme circumstances. She first sought to convince the attorney that even a drop in the market would not necessarily hurt the price that the painting commanded and pointed to the sale of van Gogh's *Irises* for $53.9 million just three weeks after the market crash in 1987. She also explained that withdrawing the painting would lessen its value because, regardless of what was said, potential buyers would attribute the withdrawal to a problem with the painting, and not the state of the financial markets.

Nonetheless, Patty also realized that she could not totally persuade him that a major collapse in the stock markets would have no effect on the sale price. So, recognizing his interest, she came up with a creative proposal. They agreed that if all three major stock markets, the New York Stock Exchange, the London FTSE, and the Japanese Nikkei fell by a certain percentage for a certain number of days, the owner could withdraw the painting. This satisfied the owner's concern while also protecting Christie's because it would have taken a major economic crisis for all three markets to fall at the same time. In fact, the Nikkei did drop by the specified amount shortly before the auction date. If Patty had agreed to allow a withdrawal based on a financial setback in any one of those markets, the auction would not have proceeded. Yet because of what they agreed to, the auction proceeded, and the painting eventually sold for $82.5 million, the most ever paid for a painting sold at auction.

The "principled negotiations" approach discussed in *Getting To Yes,* which relies on the use of objective criteria, can be used to determine which of the available criteria to select. Criteria might include fair market value, what has been done elsewhere, or the opinion of an expert. Alternatively, the parties could agree on procedures to resolve the dispute. Mothers do this all the time with their children when, for example, they have one cut the cake and the other select the piece they want. In a business dispute, for instance, each party might agree to select an expert who will give an opinion as to the appropriate outcome. If both experts agree, then the parties will abide by their decision. If they don't, the experts will select a third expert whose decision would be binding.

Principled negotiations can be viewed as a form of convincing rather than collaborating. Even if you agree in principle to base your decision on objective criteria, there will always be questions as to what criteria should be used. For every expert who says one thing, you can usually find another who will say just the opposite. Even negotiating about how to decide can be manipulated to favor the process you think will provide you with the most favorable outcome. "Objective" criteria, and experts, for that matter, are rarely neutral. Rather, they are tools we use to *convince*.

In the end, collaboration depends on your ability to develop a relationship in which the parties care not only about the substantive outcome but also how the other person feels at the end of the negotiations. The success of collaborative negotiations requires two things: that you satisfy your needs, and that those on the other side walk away feeling that they have satisfied theirs. Skillful use of all the *convince, collaborate,* and *create* techniques we discuss in this book will help you to achieve that objective.

5

> *Two roads diverged in a wood,*
> *and I took the one less traveled,*
> *and that has made all the difference.*
>
> —ROBERT FROST

Create

If You Don't Like the Rules, Change the Game—Changing the Way We Negotiate

Several years ago, a television commercial set on a basketball court in a school gym ran every Sunday morning. Boys in gym clothes are choosing up sides. The biggest, most athletic kids are picked first. At the end, two boys are left, one short with glasses and the other a little overweight. Just as the last two are being picked, a teacher walks out on to the gym floor and says, "OK, let's get ready for the spelling bee," whereupon the last two boys' faces light up. They high-five each other and yell out, "Yeah."

Each of us is better at some games than at others. Some of us like to play. Some of us don't enjoy games at all. The same is true of negotiating. *Create* is all about changing the rules of the game, changing the game itself, or figuring out a way to make it seem as if you are not negotiating at all. It is about changing the negotiating paradigm under which you are operating to one that better suits your goals or your negotiating style.

When I teach negotiating, I like to offer analogies between different types of negotiations and different games. Just as the rules for baseball differ from those for basketball or chess, so do the rules for different types of negotiations. Each "game" requires different skills and interactions. The rules in a negotiation are the expectations that the parties bring to it based on their relationship, their prior dealings, custom, and other factors. Unlike baseball, basketball, or chess, though, the rules in negotiations can be changed. Most negotiations are like playing with dolls or jumping rope, where there are no rules or you make them up as you go along. More important, not only can you change the rules, you can change the game. "This is the way we always do it" doesn't have to be the way it is done. When you *create,* you change the negotiating paradigm to one that makes you feel more comfortable, makes it easier for you to achieve your goals, or sometimes just forces everyone to take a fresh look at what is really going on. At times you need to completely change the way the negotiations are conducted. At its best, when you *create*, the parties do not view what is taking place as a negotiation at all.

DON'T BE AFRAID TO TAKE A FRESH LOOK

Recently I was teaching a class in negotiating for Women Unlimited, an organization that helps corporations to develop high-potential women executives. During the lunch break, one of the women, whom I will call "Donna," came up and asked for help. One of the assignments for the program participants was to interview their company's CEO and report back to the group. Donna had been unable to arrange a meeting with her CEO and had been rebuffed several times by the CEO's assistant, who said her boss was too busy to meet with her. Donna had already tried taking a win-win approach when the assistant had told her that the CEO didn't have time and, moreover, that if he gave an interview to her he would have to do it for others. She tried to counter those objections by suggesting that all the company-sponsored women in the program jointly interview the CEO for no more than 20 minutes. That offer was also rejected.

The assistant perceived that her job was to protect the CEO from everyone making demands on his time. As long as she considered the women in the program as just another group trying to get some of the CEO's time, she would view it as her role to prevent that from happening. So I suggested that Donna try to change the assistant's role in the negotiations by asking for her advice on how best to approach the subject of getting an interview with the CEO. By making the assistant an ally rather than an adversary, Donna was able to change the negotiating paradigm. She reported back to me that, when she approached the topic that way, the assistant offered to raise the subject again with the CEO at "an appropriate time." Eventually, with the assistant's help, Donna should be able to get the desired interview.

Most people would not think of this as a negotiation, but it is one, and approaching it that way greatly increases the likelihood of success. Using a traditional outcome-oriented negotiating approach, whether "win-win" or "zero-sum," would have failed to take into account the relationship aspect of this negotiation. This was not about the CEO's interests but about the assistant's view of her role in protecting his time. The key to success in the situation lay in changing the assistant's perception of her role from being an adversary trying to keep Donna from seeing the CEO to being an ally in helping her find a way to meet with him.

DETERMINE IF OTHERS DO IT DIFFERENTLY

Create doesn't necessarily require that you come up with a new way of dealing with a situation that no one has ever considered before. More often than not, it just requires adopting and adapting what someone else has done elsewhere or in other situations. To para-phrase NBC's clever tag line for marketing reruns, "If you haven't seen it before, it's new to you."

Soon after I joined Macy's as their Vice President of Labor Relations, I had the opportunity to use the *create* concept. The company had a good relationship and a long history of negoti-ating with its largest union, which had not had a strike against the company in over 20 years. In the past, negotiations had con-sisted of the union making numerous proposals, often in excess of a hundred, and the company responding to them one by one. Over the course of several months, the company would agree to some, tell the union why it couldn't agree to others, and com-promise on those that remained. In this game, the union always played offense and the company always played defense.

That was not how I had negotiated at other companies, nor did the company deal with its other unions that way. I didn't think it was the way to negotiate, but it was the way things had been done for the past 20 years. It took some effort to convince my colleagues that we should do something different this time, but in the end, we changed the rules and presented the union with our own list of proposals: only about a dozen, and modest ones at that. The change, though, had the intended effect. We spent at least as much time discussing our 12 proposals as the union's hundred-plus proposals. This approach allowed us to go on the offensive at times, which is more fun than always being on the defensive. Most important, the union agreed to some of our proposals, proving once again that you can't get what you don't ask for. What I did was really very simple: I merely sug-gested that we do what most other companies were already doing and what the company did when negotiating with other unions. The biggest obstacle to adopting this common sense approach was that Macy's had not done it that way with this union before. Once this new approach was adopted, however, it greatly changed how the negotiations proceeded.

Similarly, Cincinnati Bengals Executive Vice President Katie Blackburn, who handles the team's contract negotiations with players, was able to sign Peter Warrick, their top draft pick, by being creative. The NFL salary cap limits how much a team can pay players. As the fourth player picked in the NFL draft, Peter was asking for a lot of money. The team was willing to pay him a lot, but only if he performed. So both sides agreed to graduated incentives based on performance factors such as total receptions, receiving yards, and team wins. The use of incentives was not new; other teams have used them, and so have the Bengals, but it was their creative approach to using incentives that enabled them to reach an agreement well before training camp began.

Changing the way you approach negotiations works particularly well in business situations where you routinely negotiate the same type of deals. But, because each negotiation is unique in some way, you must look at each individually and not simply rely on what has been done in the past. Sometimes the key to being creative is to take certain issues out of the negotiations. In an individual negotiation you can take an issue off the table by doing what Cosmopolitan Group Publishing Director Donna Lagani refers to in Chapter 3 as "bulletproofing" a subject. At other times, you can do this by standardizing how a particular issue is handled.

Create is about changing the way you negotiate. It requires that you look at every situation with a fresh eye so you can see what will work best for you. It is not about how to slice up the pie (convince) or how to expand the pie (collaborate). It's about baking cakes instead of pies, or buying them instead of baking them yourself. You can always find a different way to go about getting what you want. All you need to do is to keep an open mind and look for new ways to approach the situation.

GET THE OTHER PARTY TO MOVE TO YOUR SIDE OF THE TABLE

Before the United States began negotiating with North Vietnam in Paris to end the Vietnam War, the two sides spent a good deal of time bargaining about the shape of the table. Would it be round or square, rectangular or oval? Obviously there was a belief that the shape of the table, as well as where the parties sat, made a difference. Experts say that working at a round or oval table tends to lead to a more cooperative negotiation, whereas working at a square or rectangular table is more adversarial. The shape of the table, however, is nowhere nearly as important as the relationship of the parties. You can accomplish much more by changing the nature of the relationship than by changing the shape of the negotiating table. One way you can create when you negotiate is to get the other party to "move to your side of the table."

A career counselor that I know had to create a new negotiating paradigm when she was faced with having to negotiate compensation with a friend. She had developed a course on coaching for the evening division of a major university. She sought my advice because she felt she was not being fairly compensated for her work, which was extremely profitable for the university. The director of the program, who was not only her boss but also a friend, had told her that she was already receiving the maximum rate for instructors and that, if they paid her more, they would have to raise the other instructors' rates as well. I suggested that she find out how much another university would pay her to teach the course and use another offer to convince the university to increase her rate of pay. If the director refused to match the offer, she could always teach the course elsewhere. My friend didn't feel comfortable doing that because of her relationship with the director. We then discussed how to change the negotiating paradigm to turn the relationship into an advantage rather than a disadvantage.

We decided that she should explain to the director how much work was involved in preparing and teaching the course, and then seek her help, as a friend, to find a way to increase her compensation. My friend did exactly that, and changed the paradigm from "asking her boss for a raise because she could command a higher salary elsewhere" to "asking a friend for advice about dealing with what she believed was an unfair situation."

After learning how much preparation was involved and how much material had to be covered, the director came up with the idea of paying her an additional fee for her extra preparation time and adding two more class sessions, for which she would be paid her hourly rate. This allowed the director to pay my friend more without affecting the pay structure of the other instructors.

This is an excellent example of how the *create* model works in conjunction with convincing and collaborating skills. My friend first had to convince the director that the compensation was not commensurate with the work involved. In addition, she had to collaborate to find a way to accommodate her interest in being paid more with the director's interest in not having to pay all the other instructors more as well. But had she not created a different negotiating paradigm, she never would have succeeded. In her previous attempts to discuss the issue, she had been told that nothing could be done since she was already at the top rate.

EXAMINE YOUR ASSUMPTIONS

To create a new negotiating paradigm, start by examining the assumptions that the parties bring to the situation. These assumptions are typically unstated, and often the parties themselves are unaware of them. Think about how similar situations have been handled in the past. Look at the relationships. Is there a boss to whom a person must answer? Will the person's spouse have a say in the agreement? Is the person doing the negotiating doing so on behalf of someone else? Once you analyze the parties' expectations of how things should proceed, you can consider all the possible ways to approach the negotiations. Examine each party's interests. Then see if you are comfortable that the approach you are taking makes sense in terms of the interests involved or whether there might be a better one.

Sometimes you won't be able to get what you want by convincing or collaborating. Then your only choices are to *create* or to walk away. In what Women In Need CEO Bonnie Stone described as the most difficult negotiation of her career, she had to negotiate with a coalition of organizations representing the severely disabled. At the time, she was Deputy Commissioner for the Human Resources Administration of the City of New York. She had been put in charge of changing the status of home health care workers caring for the disabled and elderly from independent contractors to employees to comply with federal law.

Bonnie had been on the job only two days when she attended a meeting to discuss this issue with the coalition. The leaders of this loose coalition were all physically challenged themselves. They attended in wheelchairs, with respirators, and with their attendants. Bonnie's boss, the commissioner, went through all the logical reasons why the agency had to make this change and why it would be a good thing for the coalition's constituents. The coalition leaders refused to go along with any change. The commissioner was taken aback by their response and didn't know what to do, so she set up a task force and named Bonnie to head it.

Bonnie recognized that the coalition was politically potent and could stop this project in its tracks. She realized that the members viewed the situation as a control issue because, under the proposed system, their attendants would no longer work directly for them. Most of these individuals were physically powerless: they could not feed or dress themselves and had little control over their environment. They were not about to give up one of the few things they felt they did control.

Bonnie also understood that she could not negotiate an acceptable resolution to this problem the same way she might with other advocacy groups. This group would automatically reject anything the government proposed. Worse yet, even if she could get one group to agree, it wouldn't mean anything because the coalition member groups could not agree among themselves on how to proceed. The only thing on which they all agreed was that they didn't trust the government. Once Bonnie realized this, she was able to create a new negotiating paradigm: She allowed the coalition itself to come up with the solution. In the end, the coalition decided to set up its own nonprofit corporation that then hired the home-care workers as its employees.

KEEP YOUR GOAL FIRMLY IN MIND

As long as you know what you are trying to achieve, there are any number of ways to reach your goal. Robin Tomchin, President of RT Productions, who manages the careers of jazz musicians, was working with Janis Siegel of the rock group Manhattan Transfer. Janis was trying to launch a solo career as a jazz singer. It was important for Janis to record a couple of albums to become visible as a solo artist. Robin tried to get a record label to agree to a two-album deal. Because of the state of the market, however, she couldn't find anyone to commit to more than a single-record deal. Robin therefore created a different approach that achieved the same result. She proposed that Janis do one album with an option to do a second if the first sold a certain number of records. Robin knew the market, and she anchored the required sales figure low enough that she was sure Janis would meet it. The record company agreed, and Janis sold more than enough records to ensure she would make the second album.

TRY SOMETHING DIFFERENT

Even in the simplest everyday negotiation, you can create a new negotiating paradigm if the way you are proceeding isn't working. You don't have to be a genius to do so; you just have to be willing to try something different. Investigative Consultants principal Claire Irving did just that when she couldn't get the help she needed with a recently purchased electronic organizer. The salesperson had told her that it would work with the particular program she used but that she would need to purchase additional software. He suggested that she call customer support to find out what she needed to do. When she called, the representative that answered told her that the company did not provide technical support for the software she was using. Claire recounted what the salesperson had told her and said she just wanted to know what software she needed to purchase. The customer service representative again responded that they did not support that program. They went back and forth for several minutes until Claire was ready to blow up. Then she changed the paradigm. She asked whether, if she hung up and called back, she would end up talking with him. The representative replied, "Probably not," whereupon Claire thanked him, hung up, and called back. A different customer service representative answered and quickly resolved her problem.

When Claire realized that what she was doing wasn't working, she changed the person she was negotiating with and thereby created a wholly different negotiation. This is the essence of what *create* is all about.

6

> *Women and men look at the world through very different moral frameworks. Men tend to think in terms of "justice" or absolute "right and wrong," while women define morality through the filter of how relationships will be affected.*
>
> —RON TAFFEL

Mars and Venus:
Negotiating with Men Versus Negotiating with Women

Most of the concepts discussed throughout this book apply equally regardless of whether you are negotiating with a man or with a woman. However, there are times when you need to adjust your negotiating approach depending on whether you are dealing with a man or a woman. Women tend to exhibit what we refer to as a "relational" negotiating style, while men tend to adopt a "competitive" style. Although some men favor the former and some women favor the latter, it's important to remember that each individual tends to favor one style or the other. When you can identify a person's negotiating style, you will be in a better position to determine how to best influence him or her.

NEGOTIATING STYLES: WOMEN CIRCLE, MEN GO DIRECT

When women negotiate, they tend to be less direct than men. According to psychologist Patricia Farrell, women are raised with the idea that there is a certain etiquette required to maintaining relationships. Their mothers involve them, beginning as little girls, in certain rituals such as welcoming new neighbors and sending holiday greeting cards and thank-you notes for gifts. This relationship etiquette carries over into how women negotiate.

Because of the importance women place on relationships, they want to connect on some other basis before getting down to the business of negotiating. They usually expect to talk about personal issues, such as your family or what is going on in your life. Most women would consider it rude to get down to business immediately, without first engaging in social conversation. Similarly, when actually negotiating, women tend not to go directly to the topic they want to discuss. Rather, they "circle" and take longer to get to where they want to go. Most men, on the other hand, prefer to get directly down to the business at hand, with only a minimum of small talk. When dealing with women, most men prefer that they get right to the point. When men negotiate, they first try to build credibility, then they go in for the kill. That is why men usually start off negotiations by talking about their position and their accomplishments. This is their way of establishing credibility before they get down to discussing substantive issues.

As mentioned earlier, men use relationships to get what they want, whereas women tend to value relationships for their own sake. As a result, women are more interested in working out solutions that satisfy everyone. This sometimes requires a little more time and they are willing to take it if necessary. Men, on the other hand, tend to be impatient. Once they find an acceptable solution, they are more likely to apply pressure on the other side to simply agree to it. Moreover, because women are expected to be caring, while men are expected to be self-interested, women often have to work harder to get a man to accept responsibility for the results of the negotiation and to negotiate fairly.

Men and women also communicate differently. Communicating with men is sometimes like "speaking a second language." To be successful in business, women need to understand what some of the women we interviewed refer to as "guy speak." For example, when a man leaves a meeting and you ask him how it went, he will probably say "Great." He is not really conveying any information about what happened at the meeting; rather, he is simply acting confident. A woman, in contrast, might answer the same question with, "Okay, but I could have handled the cost issue a little better." Like the man's comment, hers does not necessarily describe what happened at the meeting. Rather, it reflects her "desire for perfection." If you rely on what each actually says, without taking into account the gender of the speaker, you are liable to draw erroneous conclusions. The same is true when men and women negotiate.

The different negotiating styles men and women tend to exhibit are a natural corollary to these different communication styles. The "relational style" usually associated with women focuses on the relationship between the parties. Inherent in that negotiating style is a desire not only to achieve substantive objectives but also to develop the relationship between the two sides. The "competitive style" usually associated with men focuses more on the substantive outcome of the negotiation. Some women who are more comfortable with a relational style adopt a competitive one because they believe it to be more effective, especially in business settings. You not only need to be aware of your own style, but also you need to be able to move from one to the other depending upon whom you are negotiating with. You can determine your style by looking at the criteria in the Negotiating Style box below. Then gauge the style of those with whom you are dealing so you can recognize how they are likely to approach negotiations and prepare accordingly. Although it is important to be yourself, when you are dealing with someone whose style is different, recognize this and adjust your style as necessary. You should also make frequent use of active listening techniques to make sure the two of you are communicating.

COMPETITIVE NEGOTIATING STYLE (MALE)

- You want to get down to the business at hand as quickly as possible.
- Small talk is kept to a minimum except where it facilates the negotiation.
- Before you begin to negotiate you want to find out about your counterpart's status and make them aware of yours.
- You give weight to what people say because of the position they hold.
- A discussion is not considered successful unless you have made progress toward reaching a favorable agreement.
- Satisfying the other parties' interests is significant only to the extent that furthers your own interests.
- You want to reach an agreement as quickly and efficiently as possible.
- The outcome of this negotiation takes priority, although you take into consideration the impact your actions might have on future dealings.

RELATIONAL NEGOTIATING STYLE (FEMALE)

- You want to get to know the other person first, before you begin to negotiate.
- You would consider it rude not to talk about family and personal matters before getting down to business.
- You do not feel comfortable talking about your status and achievements because you do not want to appear to be boastful.
- The positions people occupy means less than the positions they take when negotiating and your relationship with them.
- You consider time spent establishing a better relationship to be time well spent.
- You want the other parties to feel good when the negotiations are concluded.
- You are willing to take the time necessary to satisfy everyone's needs.
- Consideration of the long-term relationship is as important as the outcome of any single negotiation.

If you are a woman negotiating with a man who favors a competitive style, you will find it effective to establish your credentials before you begin to seriously discuss the issues. You might mention people you know in common, your accomplishments, and your position, or demonstrate your expertise in the subject matter you are discussing. For example, you might introduce yourself as Sally Jones, Vice President of Development for Mega-Venture Capitalist, Inc., with a corporate mandate to find promising startups as possible investments. The man will then know your status in the organization and what you can do for him. You could follow this up with a statement like, "I believe that you know Ron Smith. I just did a deal with him in which we invested $10 million in his new magazine." By mentioning that you just finished negotiating with someone the man knows, you have not only further enhanced your credibility but have also invited him to check out your reputation as a negotiator with Ron Smith, which he will no doubt do at his first opportunity. Assuming that your relationship with Ron Smith is good, this should facilitate the negotiation.

Many women feel uncomfortable discussing their credentials because they fear being seen as boastful. But if you fail to establish that you belong at the table when you are negotiating with someone who favors a competitive negotiating style, you put yourself at a disadvantage.

BE WARY OF MEN WHO TAKE ADVANTAGE OF THE RELATIONSHIP

Sometimes men negotiating with women who have a relational style may try to manipulate the relationship to further their own interests. If you suspect this is occurring, make sure that the relationship is intended to help both parties get what they need, not to get you to give up what you want for the sake of the relationship.

If you refuse to accept any agreement that does not satisfy your interests, this tactic will not succeed.

DEALING WITH MEN WHO TREAT NEGOTIATING AS SPORT

Some men who favor a competitive style like to negotiate just to negotiate. It is sport for them. Negotiating is a competition. No matter what you agree to, it will not be enough. Very often, these men have trouble negotiating with women. It's always hard for them to lose, but losing to a woman is unthinkable. You need to recognize this "negotiation as sport" attitude and realize that you won't be able to convince this person of the fairness of your position nor will you be able to collaborate with him to find a mutually beneficial solution. Your choices are to provide him with the illusion that he has bested you, or to create a new paradigm that he will not view as a contest that he needs to win.

Ellen Sandles, Executive Director for the Tri-State Private Investors Network, found herself in just such a situation when she was forming the network. So she created a different negotiating paradigm, which did not force this individual to have to lose face. She was trying to convince a potential member to join the network but he didn't want to pay the $400 annual membership fee. The man in question was a multimillionaire who had made a fortune in mergers and acquisitions. He was a brilliant man who negotiated for a living. Ellen gave him all the logical reasons why the organization needed to charge a membership fee. He suggested other ways that the network could make money without charging a fee. They kept going back and forth until she finally realized the issue was not money. The amount involved was insignificant to this man. It was about winning—he wanted to get something no one else had gotten. So she created a new paradigm by changing the situation from a negotiation to information gathering. She said, "I'll tell you what. I haven't heard any objections from the other investors. So let me talk to them, and, if others raise similar concerns, I'll reconsider your request." After about a month, she had met her initial membership goal, and no one else had complained about the membership fee. She then sent the businessman a letter telling him that the network was having its first meeting. She told him that she had 40 members and that none had raised concerns about the membership fee. She invited him to the meeting and said that the group would love to have him join them as a member. She added that he didn't need to RSVP; all he needed to do was to show up with his check. He did, and he became one of her best members. By acting as if there had been no dispute over the fee issue but rather an agreement to abide by the consensus of the group, Ellen was able to get him to join. And, by never bringing up the fact that he had tried to negotiate a fee waiver but failed, she made sure he didn't lose face. Had she mentioned it, he probably would not have joined.

CREATING THE RIGHT RELATIONSHIP WITH MEN

As we mentioned in Chapter 2, most women are ineffective when they try to negotiate like a man, particularly when they are negotiating with a man. If you try to go head to head with a man the way another man might, it is usually counterproductive. If you challenge a man directly, you may be setting up a contest that he is likely to feel he has to win. Oxygen Media COO Lisa Hall was a college basketball player. She likens that approach to what would happen to her at the college gym when she would get into pick-up games with men she didn't know:

> Either they completely overplay you because they are afraid you'll win, or they don't bother playing you at all. Either way, it doesn't work. The same is true for negotiations.

You need to make men feel comfortable. Lisa believes you do that in business by "establishing that you are worthy of their trust, that you understand the issues, and that you are on the same playing field. That way, they don't feel the need to overplay you or ignore you."

NEGOTIATING TURN ONS FOR MEN

Getting right down to business

Letting him go first

Finding out what he is interested in

Showing that you can get the deal done

NEGOTIATING TURN OFFS FOR MEN

Whining or crying

Too much small talk

Challenging him head on

Threatening

You want the people you are negotiating with to relax. Talk about things you have in common: family, mutual friends, shared interests. Put them at ease. As mentioned in Chapter 3, this will allow them to open up and provide you with the information you need to work out a deal. This is particularly important when you are negotiating with a man. Some men are threatened by a strong woman. They may feel threatened by your intelligence or your position. Women make a mistake if they fail to recognize this when it happens. If you find yourself in this situation, adjust your style to make the man feel comfortable. Recognize his areas of expertise. Ask him questions to which he knows the answers.

Solicit his opinions, particularly in his areas of expertise. Don't set up confrontations. Get him to view you as an ally, and assure him that "you want to work with" him.

Gail Evans puts men at ease in negotiations by "trying to give in on the first question." She tries "to be amenable to his first request, which is usually a minor point. This allows him to relax. He thinks it will be easy and drops his guard. He then feels that he has to give you something in return." According to Gail, "It is better to fight on the fifth point than on the first," so I "try to hold my fire for the important points."

Employment attorney Nancy Erica Smith says, "Men can get away with threats. They can scream. Women who do that are shrill. If I am aggressive, people are turned off and can't hear me." She sometime runs into female attorneys who think that to be effective they need to be more aggressive than their male counterparts. For the reasons discussed previously, that seldom works. Nancy describes one situation in which she was representing a terminated male executive suing his former employer. The opposing counsel was a woman who had adopted an aggressive style and was badgering and disrespectful to Nancy's client. In the settlement discussions the company lawyer took very unreasonable positions. The negotiations were a disaster. The company eventually fired the woman lawyer and brought in a new lawyer. He took a totally different approach, and the case settled shortly thereafter. According to Nancy, the case probably would have settled for less, and much earlier, if the first attorney had not sought to prove how tough she was.

CREATING THE RIGHT RELATIONSHIP WITH OTHER WOMEN

Women find it more difficult to negotiate with people they dislike than men do. Experienced negotiators recognize this. So, before getting down to the actual negotiations, they will try to establish a common bond with them. Although this approach is useful with men, it is even more important when you negotiate with women. One female executive we interviewed notes that:

> When you negotiate with women it is better if you know something personal about them so you can "chat them up." That makes it easier to talk to them. It makes them more comfortable and reduces the level of contentiousness. They are flattered and feel more important. It makes it is easier to negotiate with them.

You can connect with some women just because you are both women. KPMG's Terri Santisi finds that, among female executives in the entertainment industry, there is "an automatic mutual respect when professional women negotiate with each other; whereas with a man you have to prove yourself." But you cannot assume that just because you are dealing with another woman, you will share a sense of common purpose. Many women are suspect when you approach a situation that way. The apparent bond you share is not genuine because you have not actually taken the time to develop a relationship.

NEGOTIATING TURN ONS FOR WOMEN

Taking time to find out about her

Treating her professionally

Showing respect for her point of view

NEGOTIATING TURN OFFS FOR WOMEN

Threatening

Screaming

Being sarcastic

Negotiating with other women can also be difficult if they view you as competition or feel a need to prove that they are as tough as a man. When you are faced with a woman who has a competitive negotiating style, she will probably be tougher with you because you are a woman. If you find yourself in this situation, negotiate with her as you would with anyone who has a competitive negotiating style. Establish your credentials, exhibit confidence, and be prepared to walk away if necessary.

Whether you are negotiating with men or women, keep in mind that all people are individuals. They all have their hot buttons. Find out what these are. Talk with people who know them. Learn what is important to them. Develop a relationship. Determining their negotiating style will also help you understand what they are actually saying and allow you to negotiate in a way that they can relate to. The better you understand them, the more effective you will be.

7

Next to care in choosing a partner, I should place courtesy after marriage.

—M. W. DAMROSCH

Make Every Day Valentine's Day

Getting What You Want from Your Husband or Boyfriend

We started this book with a story that Jerri DeVard, Chief Marketing Officer for Citibank's eConsumer Group, told about her son and a little girl who had quite distinct views as to the best use for a watergun. That story demonstrates how different men and women can be even at a young age. The first time I heard Jerri speak at a business conference, however, she said something that illustrates those differences even more powerfully. Someone from the audience asked her about her greatest success. She didn't point to one of her many successful marketing campaigns, as I assumed she would. Instead, without a moment's hesitation, she replied, "Choosing my husband to marry." I thought to myself that no man I knew would have answered that way. I also thought about what a good answer it was. Deciding who you'll marry may be the most important decision of your life. When it comes to negotiating successfully with your spouse, it helps to pick the right person to marry.

CHOOSE WISELY

In any negotiation, deciding whom to deal with often determines how successful the process will be. The same is true in your marriage. If finding a good fit is important when you choose an employer, how much more important is it when you choose someone with whom to share your life? It is much easier to negotiate with someone who shares your basic values and who loves and respects you, because, in a marriage, as in many other types of negotiations, if you choose the right partner, the relationship becomes more important than the outcome. And that makes negotiating easier, no matter what the issue.

However, negotiating with your spouse is unlike any other negotiation. If you don't agree, you cannot simply walk away. In addition, you and your husband probably know each other better than anyone else with whom you will ever negotiate. To complicate matters further, it is difficult, if not impossible, to take the emotion out of the situation.

NEGOTIATE RARELY

The secret to negotiating with your husband is to do it as little as possible. Women who have successful marriages have found ways to do that. If you and your partner are basically on the same wavelength regarding most issues, you will have fewer issues to negotiate. Moreover, when you do, it will be easier to find common ground. But even if you and your spouse share many values, you won't agree on everything. The trick is to avoid having to negotiate about every little issue about which you disagree.

When you negotiate in marriage, you must keep the relationship foremost in your mind because it is usually more important than the outcome in any given instance. Anything you do or say when you negotiate with your spouse may have an impact on the relationship well beyond the particular issue you are trying to resolve. How you say things when you negotiate with your husband matters. Negotiations in marriage can never be about winning, so avoid personal attacks, and focus on the issue. Still, to have a healthy relationship, you cannot always be giving in. You must feel, overall, that the relationship is balanced—that you get as much as you give. Otherwise, you will become angry or resentful.

Most of the women we interviewed who said they had successful marriages also said they rarely negotiated with their husbands because they shared basic values and had few disagreements to begin with. However, no two people agree on everything. Individuals bring different things to relationships, and it is often those differences that attract people to one another in the first place. In a marriage, it's important to appreciate and respect those differences. This will also reduce the need to negotiate.

The key to negotiating with your spouse therefore is to devise ways of resolving issues so you don't have to negotiate often and then only about important things. Contrary to what one might expect, it is the fights over unimportant things that usually destroy marriages. If, for example, you say something harsh while negotiating about something insignificant, it can cause untold damage to the relationship. If one of you loses your temper while you are discussing something important, it is easier to forgive; it hurts much more if what you are arguing about is inconsequential. Most couples can work out the things that really matter as long as they are not constantly fighting about the ones that don't.

The negotiation about how the two of you will resolve disagreements is the most important negotiation you can have with your spouse. However, the negotiation is seldom explicit. It often begins at the start of the relationship and takes place over an extended period of time. You may not even realize that this negotiation is occurring, but if it is successful, it will serve as the foundation for a good marriage.

When discussing how they resolve most everyday issues without negotiating, most of our interviewees, remarkably, describe the same process. Typically, each partner takes responsibility for certain decisions. These decision-making responsibilities generally correspond to each spouse's perceived areas of expertise. One might take responsibility for the finances, while the other might take responsibility for the couple's activities. In other matters, each would defer to the spouse who cared most about the particular issue. Some couples also defer making a decision if they can not agree, because a matter will often resolve itself if you just keep the lines of communication open and give it some time before making a decision.

Oxygen Media COO Lisa Hall and her husband have adopted this basic approach. According to Lisa, "We both have strong personalities and we really need to divide things based on who cares the most about something. Each of us gets to call the shots about the things that are important to us." When they discuss something, it is usually obvious who cares most about it. For example, he cares about their car, so he gets to pick it. She usually makes the weekend plans because she cares more about where they go and what they do in their leisure time than he does. Both really care about their kids, so when it comes to issues concerning them, they "respect each other's expertise." If they disagree, they shelve the discussion until they can find a neutral time when things are not "emotionally charged" and try to find a compromise. The collaborative techniques of trading, expanding the pie, coupling interests, and identifying other ways to satisfy everyone's interests discussed in Chapter 4 can be very useful in resolving these situations.

Author Jean Hollands describes a situation she encountered as a marriage counselor working with a couple who had been married for 37 years but had never gone on a successful vacation together. They were about to go on their dream vacation, an African safari, and sought Jean's help. She gave them one simple piece of advice that made an enormous difference: to take turns deciding anything on which they disagreed throughout the trip. If they both wanted to do something, they would do it, but if they disagreed, they would take turns deciding. In keeping with that approach, each would be responsible for the itinerary on alternating days. For example, on Monday he would decide what they would do and where they would eat. On Tuesday, it was her turn. When they returned home, they could not thank Jean enough. It was the best trip they ever had. Both did things they would not otherwise have done— and enjoyed them.

The technique Jean suggested is a form of the "coupling interests" technique discussed in Chapter 4. If a single decision about what to do is too difficult to resolve, you couple it with future decisions and agree to take turns deciding. The same technique can be used to resolve other issues that arise in marriages and is particularly useful for dealing with recurring issues. For example, if your husband likes to eat Chinese food when you go out but you prefer Italian, you can use a 50-50 approach and simply alternate. A better approach might be what Jean refers to as "one-third, one-third, one-third"—that is, one week you go out for Italian, the next week you eat Chinese, and the third week you try something different. That allows you to work on negotiating where to eat the third week, and you can fall back on alternating who chooses if you cannot agree.

Problems can arise if the solutions that couples devise to share decision-making result in either partner feeling that the relationship is too one-sided. If you find yourself giving in or going along too often, you may need to renegotiate the decision-making process in your marriage. Just as the way you make decisions as a couple initially developed over time, often without your realizing it was occurring, the process can be changed the same way. When you renegotiate certain issues, you are in essence renegotiating the relationship. Changes to your decision-making process as a couple do not occur in the abstract. The couple described above renegotiated how they made decisions in the context of a vacation, but they did more than that. Rest assured that when they disagree about other matters now, they will use what worked for them on that vacation and take turns making decisions. That is how you renegotiate decision-making arrangements—one decision at a time.

When you decide that it is necessary to renegotiate your relationship, do so in the context of an issue that is important to you. If you have spent the last three Christmases with your husband's family and you want to spend this Christmas with yours, use the *convince, collaborate,* and *create* techniques we have discussed to get him to agree. Focus on what it will take to convince him and what is in it for him. This may be something as simple as an appeal to fairness or offering to spend New Year's with his family. Or it may be telling him that, although you care about what he wants, you are going to spend Christmas with your family this year whether he chooses to go with you or not. The one-third, one-third, one-third approach works particularly well in this instance; you could propose this Christmas at your parents, next Christmas at his parents and the following Christmas in Hawaii (where your husband can play golf). Keep in mind, however, that you are redefining the relationship. This type of change does not come easily to most people. So be certain that both the immediate issue and changing the nature of the relationship are important enough to you that you can remain resolute in your position and withstand any discomfort or even anger that may result.

COMMUNICATE OFTEN

It is no secret that to have a good marriage, you must be able to communicate with your spouse. If you don't talk with each other, if you don't share things, then something major is missing in the marriage. In a few short paragraphs, we cannot teach you how to share your innermost feelings with your husband or how to get him to share his with you. What we can tell you is: while you should rarely negotiate with your spouse, you should always communicate. If something is bothering you, don't ignore it. Resentment will build up, and it will hurt your marriage.

Use the active listening techniques discussed in Chapter 3 to work out issues that arise in the marriage. Look at things from his perspective. Let your husband know how much his efforts in the relationship mean to you, and remember to show your appreciation for the things that you love about him. If you do, you'll be more successful in negotiating for things that are important to you. For example, let's say that your husband thinks you cannot afford it, but you really want your daughter to experience summer camp. You can start out by acknowledging that camp costs a lot of money and then offer ideas for saving money elsewhere, such as taking a less expensive family vacation.

Much of the negotiating in a marriage is not explicit but rather merely an effort to keep the relationship in balance. With that in mind, take note when you compromise on an issue that is important to your husband. Then, when you want him to do the same for you, you can gently mention it. You will be surprised how effective this can be. Whenever you do that, you may want to write it down so you remember the compromises you have made when the time comes to ask for something you want.

It's also important to know what's negotiable with your husband and what isn't, and how to approach various issues. As CNN anchor Jan Hopkins notes: "No doesn't necessarily mean no. It may just mean that this is not the right time to deal with the issue, or that you are not going about it in the right way." Think through what is important to your husband. You have to be willing to work through issues and give up on some things. You should expect the same in return.

NEGOTIATING RESPONSIBILITIES: YOUR TURN TO DO THE LAUNDRY

If you find yourself resenting doing most of the housework, even though both of you work full time, talk about it. Don't harp on it. Don't nag. Use the *convince, collaborate,* and *create* techniques to work something out. Find a quiet time when the children are not around, and talk about the issue. Prepare for your discussion by making a list of all the things you do for your husband and the things that are most important to him. Then list all the chores around the house and how often they need to be done. These then become the subject of negotiation.

As the two of you talk, pay attention to his responses and keep his interests firmly in mind. You might use a *convince* approach and ask him to handle some of the chores by appealing to his sense of fairness. You might use *collaborate* and offer him the opportunity to play more golf or to visit your mother less often. Along the same lines, you might suggest that you would feel a lot more romantic if you were less overwhelmed with housework. Or you might try to *create* by suggesting that, instead of reallocating the work between the two of you, you hire someone to help with the housework. As you would in any other negotiation, approach this subject from his perspective. Whatever you agree to, be specific. If your husband agrees to do the dishes on Tuesdays, Thursdays, and Sundays, they will get done, at least most of the time. If he agrees only that he will do them three days a week, more often than not his response will be, "I'll do them tomorrow." By being explicit about your agreements, you can avoid future arguments and negative feelings. Although not every spouse will respond to this approach, these techniques can bring you surprising and satisfactory results.

NEGOTIATING LOVE: GETTING WHAT YOU WANT IN THE BEDROOM

When it comes to sex, as with anything else, you must be willing to talk about what you want. Don't expect your husband to be able to read your mind. After all, he hasn't up to this point, or you wouldn't need to have this discussion. The need to discuss sex, however, does not mean it is an easy conversation to have. Sex is a sensitive subject. Where the male ego is involved—and it always is when the topic is sex—there is tremendous potential to hurt your partner and the relationship. Most men want to be good lovers. In fact, most men think they are. But unlike how men generally learn other skills, they seldom have a knowledge-able teacher to instruct them in the art of making love. Most learn to make love through trial and error, often with someone who is no more knowledgeable than they are. For some, their first partner is their spouse. To make things more difficult, not only do men and women differ physiologically and emotionally when it comes to sex, each person is different. People respond differently to various stimuli. Your spouse may not know exactly what you want; by the same token you may not fully understand what he desires.

You can approach this issue by collaborating, convincing, or creating or a combination all three approaches. You can negoti-ate while you are actually making love. If you approach this "negotiation" collaboratively, from the perspective of your hus-band's interests, you will recognize that this may be the time when he is most motivated to satisfy you so he can be sure his interests are satisfied. Suggest what you would like him to do.

When he does something that is particularly pleasing, let him know, and show that you appreciate what he is doing. In return, try to do what he desires. Both of you should feel comfortable with whatever shared activities you choose. If you become uncomfortable, you should say so—but how you say it will make all the difference in the world. When you do say no, do so in a way that focuses on your feelings and is not judgmental or critical of what he wants.

You can also discuss the issue directly. First, try to figure out what the real issue is. Why has it arisen at this moment? Is sex really the issue, or are problems with the children or money spilling over into the bedroom? If the real problem is something else, deal with it. If it is about sex, then you may decide that the best approach is to talk about it. But don't just bring up the subject and expect to discuss it right then and there. Give your husband some time. You might say something like, "I've noticed that you don't seem to be as interested in making love as you used to be. I've got some concerns as well. So why don't we sit down and talk about it? When would be good time?" Your husband will probably try to avoid that discussion. He may deny that there is a problem or even become defensive and insist on discussing it that instant. If you can, though, try to get him to agree on a specific time and place to discuss the subject. Pick a time when it will be quiet and no one else will be around. Then, when the time comes, don't let him find an excuse to postpone the discussion.

Start by asking him about his feelings and what he sees as the problems. Use your active listening skills. Once he knows that you are open to hearing him, he will be more willing to listen to you. At some point, you must be willing to tell him exactly what you want and what the problems are from your perspective. You can do that gently, but you do need to put the issues on the table. Remember, if you don't ask for it, you won't get it. Be prepared to use all the various *convince* and *collaborate* techniques we have discussed. Your spouse may react by raising even more issues about what you are not doing for him, but do not allow yourself to become emotional or defensive.

When you have both finished describing what you see as the problems, see if there is anything you can agree on. Are there things you would both like to try, or things that you would prefer not to do? Decide when you want to work on what you have discussed. Perhaps you might want to go away for a weekend or plan to have a nice dinner beforehand. Don't expect to fix everything with just one discussion. The next time you make love, show that you appreciate your husband's efforts to improve your relationship. Keep in mind that there may be some level of performance anxiety whenever you try something new. Be supportive and understanding, try to make it fun for both of you, and don't give up if things don't work perfectly the first time.

Finally you might want to try to *create* a new paradigm when you are negotiating in this arena. You might buy a book on the subject and read it together, or try something very different and see how he responds. One couple I know bought a book on Tantric sex, which provided them with a framework to explore each other's desires. Stripped of all the spiritual Eastern elements, which may appeal to some of you and with which others will be uncomfortable, Tantric sex is nothing more than a method of having each of you take turns exploring the other's body. It provides a structured way to learn what each of you find pleasurable. While you are sexually exploring your partner's body, they are expected to tell you what they like.

Negotiating a better sex life is partly about communicating, partly about reciprocating, and partly about being creative. When you think about it that way, it is nothing more than a variation on other types of negotiating. Finally, depending on your relationship and the depth of the problem, you might even consider having this discussion with a marriage counselor or other professional.

BOYFRIENDS ARE NOT HUSBANDS

Negotiating with a boyfriend is different from negotiating with a husband. How you approach the situation will depend on where you are in that relationship. You can generally get just about anything you want early in a relationship because most men are trying to impress you and are trying to make you happy. If they do not behave that way at the start of the relationship, it is unlikely that they ever will. Assuming that he treats you well, do not take advantage of him or take his actions for granted.

>When you show that you appreciate his attention, it will continue. As a woman I have always found that if you stop showing appreciation those efforts will cease. Moreover, showing your appreciation makes future negotiations easier. The more you let your boyfriend know that you appreciate his efforts to make you happy, the more issues like where to go to dinner, what movie to see, and whose friends to spend time with will be resolved the way you would like.

Relationships require give-and-take. You cannot always get your own way. But, neither of you should feel that you are giving more than you get. Healthy, mature men are seldom attracted to women who do not stand up for themselves. If you are perceived as a "pushover," you will destroy any chance of being able to successfully negotiate with your boyfriend in the future.

Use the three keys to successful negotiating to guide you when you negotiate with your boyfriend: be confident, be prepared, and always be willing to walk away. Confidence is one of the most attractive qualities any person can have. It is just as important when you are dating as it is in business. We all have insecurities in our personal lives—even more so than in our professional lives. The key, in dating as in other negotiations, is to not let them show. If you exude confidence, men won't notice your imperfections. However, your own insecurities will magnify any flaws, if you let them, so act confident. Smile. Be friendly. Don't be afraid to talk to new people. This will multiply your options when it comes to dating, and as in any other negotiation, the more options you have, the more confident you will feel.

Confidence is key. The confidence-building technique suggested by psychologist Patricia Farrell, to psych yourself up with a little mental pep talk before negotiating, works particularly well when you are dealing with a boyfriend. Make a mental list of everything you do for him and the things that make you special. Remember, he is already attracted to you; otherwise, he would not have been interested in the first place. Figure out which of your qualities he finds most attractive—your sense of humor, your intelligence, your ability to get along with his friends, or whatever makes him want to be with you—and accentuate those qualities when you are with him. This will not only remind him why he likes you but will also give you the confidence you need to ask for, and feel entitled to get, what you want.

Figuring out what you want in a boyfriend is equally important. What qualities are you looking for? What values are important to you? Look for men who share them. You need not share all the same interests, but if you don't share basic core values, you'll find it difficult to negotiate in the relationship. You'll find yourself spending too much time negotiating or giving in too often just to maintain the relationship. Neither is healthy.

Being prepared in a relationship also means knowing what you want and why you want it. It is difficult enough for two people to work out the issues that inevitably arise in a relationship when they both want different things. When either or both of them do not know what they want, it is virtually impossible. This does not mean being insistent or demanding, which will not help any relationship. Knowing what you want and what is important to you, being flexible about the details, and being able to communicate without getting emotional will create an environment conducive to working out any problem. Believing that you deserve what you are asking for is the best way to get it.

RATION YOUR EMOTIONS

Although it helps to remain detached when you negotiate, it is almost impossible to eliminate emotions when you are negotiating with a boyfriend or husband. Emotions drive relationships in the first place. Use them to your advantage. When it comes to displaying emotions, consider "violating expectations." If you habitually cry or scream, your boyfriend will not take you seriously. He will also find your behavior irritating. If, on the other hand, you reserve displays of strong emotions for times when you are truly upset, he will take you very seriously indeed.

>─┤◆─○─◆┤─<

As a woman, particularly at the start of a relationship, I tend to keep my feelings to myself. So when I do show emotions it has a huge impact. I can remember one instance where I was having one of those days when nothing seemed to go right. My boyfriend had already made plans to go out with his friends that evening. All I had to do was let him hear in my voice how upset I was to get him to stop by on his way out. Once he was there, an unintended tear caused him to cancel his plans and take me out. My emotions were genuine, and because I rarely let them show they were incredibly powerful. But had I cried on a regular basis he probably would not even have come over. He even commented that in the eight months that he had known me, this was the first time he had ever seen me cry.

>─┤◆─○─◆┤─<

Before negotiating with your boyfriend, try to put yourself in his shoes. Figure out what he might want that would balance what you are requesting. Determine what might convince him that your request is reasonable. Play out a few possible scenarios in your head. Prepare for how he might react so you can neutralize any emotional response. Be careful not to make him feel that you are trying to manipulate him. No one enjoys being manipulated or being taken advantage of. You can avoid that by making sure that his interests are being satisfied along with your own.

SOME BOYFRIENDS ARE NOT MEANT TO BE HUSBANDS, AT LEAST NOT YOURS

When you are dating, you must be willing to walk away. If you are not, you will not be able to negotiate effectively. More importantly, you will end up in the wrong relationships. Dating is an opportunity to find out what is important to you in a relationship—what is worth compromising on and where you draw the line. It is a time to find someone with whom you can have a special relationship. It is an opportunity to see how the two of you negotiate and whether you can work together to resolve issues. If you discover that you are with the wrong person, walk away. Knowing what you want, or at least what you don't want, will enable you to make the right decisions.

It is inevitable that you will date men with whom you cannot negotiate or with whom you find yourself giving in or negotiating about everything. Avoid dating such men; you have little chance for a lasting relationship with them. Dating gives you insight into how things will be for the two of you in the long run, so pay attention to how you work out your differences—if the relationship fails to go well in its early stages, it rarely gets better.

> One time after a heated argument with a relatively new boyfriend, I told him "It's over. I am throwing in the towel." To dramatize my point, I actually picked up a towel, threw it at him, and left. Later on that night he called to apologize, and for a short while the relationship improved. Of course, when the same problems keep recurring, it is a clear signal that you are with the wrong person. When that happens, you should be willing to walk away, which is what I did with that boyfriend. No matter how much time you spent trying to build a relationship, if it is not working you need to break it off.

After you know the person you are dating well and have developed a relationship, you can use many of the same negotiating approaches that you would use if you were married. Work out ground rules for resolving disagreements. Defer to him in areas that are more important to him than to you or in which he has greater expertise. But make sure he reciprocates.

MARRIAGE: IF HE DOESN'T OFFER, BE WILLING TO WALK AWAY

Leil Lowndes, author of *How to Make Anyone Fall in Love with You,* recognizes that to be successful in business, you have to be willing to walk away. When it comes to love she recommends the same approach. When asked what advice she would offer a woman whose boyfriend was reluctant to get married, she recalled the classic Greek play *Lysistrata.* In that play, the women of the warring Greek city-states got together and agreed to withhold sex from their husbands until the men put an end to their fighting. If the time has long since passed for your boyfriend to ask you to marry him, Leil suggests:

> ...[w]ithout harping on it, you let your boyfriend know that you would like to get married. If he doesn't respond, make things really wonderful for him. Then, after a while, if he still doesn't feel that he can commit, explain that it isn't fair to either of you to continue and you should both be free to seek someone to whom you can commit.

Then, Leil advises, "Walk away. Refuse to talk to him, don't see him, and don't take his calls. If he does not propose, he probably never would have anyway."

Many of you wouldn't want to marry a man who needed that much encouragement to pop the question. Sometimes, though, you do need to force the issue. Being confident in what you have to offer and being willing to walk away will help you to get what you want. For three years, Working Mother Media President and COO Carol Evans had been dating the man she wanted to marry. But she wanted children, and he was hesitant. Her friends warned her to stop talking about children because it was scaring him. She did not take their advice because she was not about to marry him unless he also wanted children. Instead, she told him what a great father he would make and gave him a six-month deadline, until New Year's Day to decide if he wanted to marry her. She also told him she did not want to talk him into anything and that she would not mention it again. On October 31, at a Halloween party, he announced to all their friends that they were going to get married.

In the end, if your boyfriend does not want to marry you, then you have to be willing to walk away, not because he won't marry you but because he is not the right person for you. The ability to do that will not only make you more attractive to him, but to others as well.

Love is not about negotiating, but living with someone and getting along with them is. Early on, work out a way to resolve issues that is fair to both of you and doesn't require you to constantly negotiate with each other. If you do, you won't have to negotiate often, and when you do, it won't be difficult.

8

Negotiating with Your Family

If You Can Negotiate with a Two-Year-Old, You Can Negotiate with Anyone

Negotiating with your children is not much different from negotiating with anyone else. Most of the time, if you treat them with the same respect that you would a friend or business associate, you will succeed not only in the negotiation itself but also in maintaining a healthy relationship with them. You can see this even when you negotiate with very young children. For example, when *Cosmopolitan* Group Publishing Director Donna Lagani negotiates with her four-year-old son, she uses the same techniques she uses in business. She sets expectations way in advance. She tells him that "you are going to bed after your favorite television program." She gets him to agree: "Now, when this show is over, you will go to bed, right? Do we have a deal? Let's shake on it." Then she reminds him along the way: "You know this show will be over in a few minutes and that you are going to bed. Right?" And when it is time to go to bed, he goes to bed.

JUST ONE MORE SHOW, THEN I'LL DO MY HOMEWORK

There is one crucial difference when you negotiate with your children. You are ultimately responsible for their well-being and safety. Therefore, sometimes you simply have to say no. In those instances, you must be willing to assert your authority as the parent. No matter how persuasive your eight-year-old may be, you are not going to let her stay out by herself until three o'clock in the morning.

Often the problem is not that parents are unwilling to say no; it is that they say it too readily. Because you ultimately have the power to dictate the outcome when you negotiate with your children doesn't mean that you should use it. Any negotiation with a child that ends with your saying, "Because I said so!" does nothing to help your child develop confidence, judgment, or the ability to negotiate. It is better to allow children broad latitude in negotiating with you, particularly as they get older.

If you are going to negotiate with your children, you must also be willing to compromise with them. Don't just tell them no. Give them choices. Let them propose options. Teach them that their opinion is valuable. Try not to make big issues out of little ones. If your six-year-old wants to wear striped pants with a checked shirt, you can suggest another combination, but if she insists you might want to let her go ahead and wear it.

Children need to know that certain things are negotiable and others are not. Going to school and getting good grades may not be negotiable. On the other hand, curfews—staying out past curfew on a special occasion, what time their curfew is, or even whether they have a curfew—may well be issues you are willing to negotiate. If you are consistent, children will respect the lines you draw, and you will avoid a lot of unnecessary fighting. If, however, you do not allow them to negotiate about some things, they will never develop the skills and confidence they need to do so later in life. Moreover, your relationship will suffer, particularly as they grow older.

One way to teach your child negotiating skills, as well as other values, is to negotiate an allowance. Many parents simply assign their children certain chores and give them an allowance. When Jessica was growing up, we agreed that she would do certain chores around the house. In return, she received a certain allowance out of which she was expected to pay for her lunches, movies, treats, and anything else she wanted. Periodically she sought to renegotiate the amount, and I used the opportunity to allow her to convince me why her allowance should be raised. Sometimes we negotiated about her adding other chores in return for an increase. What chores she was expected to do and what she would get in return in the form of an allowance were subjects open to negotiation. That exercise taught her valuable lessons.

> **Lee:** When Jessica started babysitting, I tried to use the opportunity to teach her more about negotiating. I suggested that she find out the going rate for babysitting and ask for it from the parents. That is a hard thing for any young girl to do, but learning to ask is an important lesson that I wanted to teach her.
>
> **Jessica:** I guess that by then I had already learned how to "break the rules." I knew instinctively that it was better to let the other side make the first offer, so instead of asking for a specific rate, I told the parents to pay me "whatever they thought was appropriate." Of course, it was always at least as much as, and usually more than, the going rate. I guess that if anyone had ever offered me less than the going rate, I would have simply asked for more.

Sometimes, you may find it helpful to involve a third party. In your discussions with your children, they will often listen to advice from an aunt or a family friend that they would ignore if it came from their parents. You can use friends and relatives the same way that you might use an expert in a business negotiation. For example, when Jessica's younger sister Samantha was having trouble in school, I asked Jessica to talk to her. Both her mother and I had spoken to Samantha, to no effect, but she looks up to her sister. So when Jessica gave her some ideas about how she could do better in school, she took them seriously.

When you negotiate with your children, you must be able to listen to them. That may not always be easy because of all the emotions that come into play. You have to deal not only with their emotions but with your own as well. You have a different perspective on life than they do. To a teenager, everything is life and death. How many times have you heard your teenage daughter say, "If you don't let me do this, I'll just die." To you the issue may seem unimportant. Ten years from now, you'll both have forgotten whether you let her stay out until midnight or not. But to her, at that moment, it's the most important issue in the world. She honestly believes that whether or not you allow her to go somewhere or do something will have a major impact on her life. This doesn't mean that you have to let children do what they want, but you do need to understand how they feel.

Elaine Conway, Director of the New York State Commission on Women, says it well: "Learn how to deal with children on their level. If you start from where they are, it will be easier to get to where you want to go." Determine what their interests are. Why is this important to them? Is it peer pressure? Is it about status? Is it about independence? You have made mistakes that you don't want them to repeat. You want to protect them and not see them get hurt. They, on the other hand, are exploring. They are testing. They are learning. Allow them to make mistakes, provided that their safety and well-being are not jeopardized.

Encouraging children to be advocates for their positions will foster their negotiating skills. Ask them to explain why they want something. If you have a problem with what they are asking for, have them suggest alternatives. Try to remember what was important to you when you were young. Again, ultimately you have the power to say no and sometimes you have no choice but to assert that power. Doing what they want may not be in their best interest, and you may not be able to convince them of that. This situation commonly arises with teenagers when their friends are allowed to do things that you feel are inappropriate. However, that is often exactly when you should be negotiating with them. That is when they most need to feel that, even though you disagree, you are taking their feelings into account.

Show your child the same respect you would if you were negotiating with a stranger. Try to take the emotion out of the situation. Take a deep breath. Don't react on the spot. Give yourself some time to reflect. Allow your child some time to prepare. Set a time aside to discuss the issue in a quiet place where you will not be interrupted. Then listen, and use the same negotiating techniques you would use with anyone else. Avoid being condescending, especially when dealing with teenagers. Treat their views with respect and don't talk down to your children, no matter what their age. It also helps to acknowledge their feelings. You can say things like, "I understand how hard you are working," or "I understand why you think this is so important." If you listen to your children and can convince them that you understand their position, that is often all they are looking for. In most cases, you will be able to work out a solution that is acceptable to everyone.

G.G. Michelson tells of negotiating with her daughter, then 17, who wanted to travel through Europe with a friend for the summer. As part of that trip, she wanted to visit the then-Soviet Union. G.G. and her husband were concerned about the risks. Her daughter, of course, felt she could handle anything that arose. It was a very difficult negotiation. G.G. found it hard to keep emotions out of it. They all sought, however, to achieve some common ground. They talked about what she would do in an emergency. They agreed on an itinerary, with the understanding that if it changed she would let them know immediately. They agreed that she would check in with people whom G.G. knew in Europe. In the end, the other girl got sick during the trip and what they had negotiated proved helpful to their daughter, who had people available to assist them when problems arose.

When you are negotiating with your children, your most difficult task is to remain emotionally detached. Most issues get blown out of proportion in the heat of the moment. When that happens, take a moment to think about what is going on in the world. Then ask yourself if the issue is really that important. Then you will probably be able to deal with it in a less emotional manner.

TEACH YOUR DAUGHTERS TO NEGOTIATE

Do not approach negotiating with your children as an exercise in power, because ultimately you have the power. There is nothing wrong with offering to read your child a story if she brushes her teeth. There is nothing wrong with her asking for two stories. Whether you agree to read her two stories or only one, she is learning an important lesson: that you do not lose anything by asking. Children need to learn not only how to make good decisions for themselves but also how to get others to help them implement those decisions. One of your goals should be to teach your children how to be persuasive and influence situations. They learn by watching you and by negotiating with you. Let your daughters see you negotiate. Take them to work with you. Encourage your husband to do the same. Many of the women we interviewed commented that their fathers used to take them along when they worked and that they frequently had the opportunity to watch them negotiate.

Marcia Lite recalls negotiating with her eight-year-old son about where he would store a toy he wanted for his birthday. The toy consists of numerous pieces that could be assembled to make buildings, bridges, and other objects. The boy wanted to keep it in his room, but Marcia preferred a corner in the basement so she wouldn't trip over his creations every time she went into his room. Marcia explained why she thought the basement made more sense. In an effort to compromise, he suggested keeping it at his dad's house. Marcia had no problem with that but reminded him that he spent only every other weekend there. In the end, he decided to keep the toy in the basement, but had he decided to put it in his room, Marcia would have let him. To her where he kept his toy is less important than teaching him to make good decisions for himself and to negotiate to make those decisions a reality.

Jerri DeVard, chief marketing officer for Citibank's eConsumer Group, talks about "teachable moments." These are the opportunities we have as parents to talk about "doing the right thing" with our children. This is how they develop judgment. When she talks with her children at the dinner table about what happened during the day she uses questions to teach them. She will ask questions like, "How do you feel about what happened?," or "How do you think the other child feels?," or "What could you have done differently?" Her purpose is to teach them to think critically and to understand where others are coming from—skills that are essential for an effective negotiator.

If you give children things without their having to negotiate and earn them, they can grow up with a sense of entitlement that may keep them from being good negotiators. If you expect to get your way all the time, there is no reason to negotiate. One way to avoid that is to expose your children to lots of different types of people. The more they have to deal with all types of people, the more they will have to negotiate and the less likely they will be to always get their way.

Susan Medalie, Executive Director of The Woman's Campaign Fund, offered an excellent illustration of this. Her granddaughter had asked her father to buy her a "Glenda the Good Witch" doll. He told her he would but that she would have to wait until her birthday. Although she really wanted the doll, she did not cry or nag. A few days later, though, she came home with the doll. When her father asked where she had gotten it, she said she traded for it with another little girl in her class. She had been creative and found a different way to get what she wanted. Some parents would have made her give it back. Her father did not. He called the other girl's parents to make sure it was all right with them, then he let her keep the doll and praised her for doing what she had done.

When children negotiate with siblings or with other children, it is part of their learning process. It should be encouraged. As long as children negotiate fairly, they should not be deprived of the benefits of what they negotiate. Even when they negotiate poorly, you should not interfere. Rather, use these situations as opportunities to teach them. It is better for them to learn from small mistakes when they are young than to suffer the consequences of making those same mistakes as adults. If you do not encourage your children to negotiate, they will not develop the confidence they need, not only to negotiate but also to be successful in life. The importance of instilling confidence in our children, particularly our daughters, cannot be overstated. It may be the single most important determinant of their ultimate success in life.

9

How to Succeed in Business

Equal Pay for Equal Work—But Not Unless You Negotiate for It

Howard Stern's humor notwithstanding, women, on average, still earn only 73 cents for every dollar a man earns. Although some of that difference can be explained by differences in age, education, years on the job, hours worked, and choice of occupations, somewhere between 11 and 40 percent of the difference cannot be accounted for by those factors. Some of the difference, no doubt, is the result of discrimination. However, a significant part of that difference results from women either not negotiating, or asking for too little when they negotiate compensation.

Maxine Hartley is a longtime executive recruiter and the former President of Pearl Management, a company founded to provide venture capital for female entrepreneurs. When she was interviewed for this book, she started off by talking about a female friend who came to her seeking advice. Her friend had been offered the executive director position at a nonprofit organization in New York City. She wanted the job but was unhappy with the salary being offered. Maxine had her put together a list of four items that would make the package more attractive to her. Her friend lived in New Jersey, so first on the list was to get the organization to pay for her commuting costs and parking. The nonprofit also owned an apartment in the city that she wanted to be able to use when she needed to stay over. A signing bonus was then added to the list. Rounding off the list was an early performance review. Any one or two of these items would have more than offset the low salary she was being offered. The friend presented her list to the board of directors not as demands but as requests that she thought were reasonable in light of the position she was being offered. In the end, the nonprofit agreed to several of her requests, and she accepted the job. When negotiating compensation, the only way to be certain you get what you deserve is to know your market worth, to firmly and creatively negotiate a compensation package consistent with that market value, and to be willing to walk away if you do not get it.

IT NEVER HURTS TO ASK

Compare Maxine's advice to her friend with what she describes as her own worst negotiation. She was a young human resources executive being interviewed for a job with a company in Atlanta. She was flown down for several interviews. She liked the company and they wanted to hire her. She spent a lot of time talking with the company about compensation. In the end, she didn't go to work for them because of the money. She was looking for a salary of at least $50,000 a year. Ultimately, they only offered her $40,000. When they made her the offer, she didn't ask for anything else. She didn't negotiate. Instead, she simply refused the offer. Today, she says, she would have tried to bridge the gap by asking for any number of things such as a signing bonus or a raise once she achieved certain agreed-upon objectives. When we asked her why she had not done that then, she replied, "It never occurred to me to negotiate." Although men sometimes just accept what is offered as well, they usually see an offer as the starting point for negotiations. Women, on the other hand, are much more likely to simply accept the first offer a potential employer makes. Women too seldom negotiate when considering a job offer, and, even when they do, women usually ask for too little.

This is not an issue only for young women seeking their first job. Cathleen Black, President of Hearst Magazines, noted that even experienced businesswomen sometimes fail to ask for commensurate compensation when they are given additional responsibilities or are promoted. When asked why, she quoted something Gloria Steinem had told her when they were working together at *Ms.* magazine in the 1970s: "Women have a terminal case of gratitude." In other words, women tend to be flattered by the mere offer of employment and are afraid to do anything that might jeopardize it. Often, this rules out the possibility of asking for anything else. If a woman is really interested in a job, she usually accepts with little, if any, negotiating. Fortunately, this is not as true today as it was 30 years ago because women today are coming into the workplace with greater confidence in their ability and a greater sense of self-worth. Although it is normal to appreciate being given an opportunity, you have a right to be compensated appropriately. But you should expect to have to ask. If you do not, you probably won't be paid what you deserve.

Employers expect all but entry-level hires (and, in recent years, sometimes even those) to negotiate. Therefore, they almost never start with their best offer—so if you do not negotiate, you will probably be accepting less than the employer was prepared to pay. This is not only a mistake initially; it is one that will continue to be compounded over the years, disadvantaging you throughout the remainder of your career. Every raise you get, every bonus you receive, and even the number of stock options you are awarded, will be smaller because these amounts are normally determined as a percentage of your artificially low base salary.

Many women think they will accept a job, prove themselves, and then ask for a raise. This approach may result from believing that you are not in a position to negotiate, from being afraid that, if you ask for more, you might lose the job offer, from being uncomfortable negotiating, or simply from thinking that it is the most effective approach. Whatever the reason, in most instances, you will be wrong. Once you prove yourself in a job, you will be able to get even more money, over and above what you negotiate at the time you initially accept a job. By not negotiating at the outset, you are not only forgoing the money you could have gotten but also reducing the amount of the raise you will get after you prove yourself. Imagine that you could have initially negotiated a salary $5000 higher than the one you accepted without negotiating. When you get that 10 percent raise because you are doing such a great job, it will be based on your lower, unnegotiated salary—and will be $500 less than it would have been if you had negotiated in the first place, and your hard-earned first raise will still leave you earning $5500 less than if you had originally negotiated and then received the raise you deserve.

Employers may actually think less of you if you do not negotiate. They may even become concerned that you will not be able to negotiate effectively with vendors and customers. When Davia Temin was offered the position of head of strategic marketing at General Electric Capital Services, she had very little experience negotiating compensation. Although she had been extremely successful in her career and had negotiated many business deals, she had never negotiated her own compensation. In the past, when offered a new position, she had approached it as a choice: If she liked the offer, she accepted it; if not, she turned it down. This position, however, was at a whole different level. She would be on the management committee of one of the largest companies in the industry. Davia realized there were a lot of things that she could ask for, but she didn't know where to begin. So she sought advice from a friend. He advised her to ask for more money, a signing bonus, stock options, and a contract. She was nervous that they "would be mad at me for negotiating and they wouldn't like me," but she took her friend's advice. To her surprise, they not only responded well, but it was obvious that they had expected her to negotiate. After all, she would have to negotiate on their behalf once she was in the job. The moral of this story is: Don't be afraid to negotiate. Davia not only got what she asked for but also earned the respect of her employer in the process.

KNOW YOUR OWN WORTH

When it comes to negotiating compensation, information is power. Determine what your skills and experience are worth in the market, and do not accept less. Your current salary will normally weigh heavily in determining the amount you receive. If you are being paid below market value, and the company bases its offer on your current compensation, this will work to your disadvantage. For this reason, it is important to anchor salary discussions based on market value rather than on your current salary. To do that, you must know the range of salaries being paid to others with similar skills and experience.

Salary information is readily available today. A number of Internet Web sites provide salary information. The Riley Guide at rileyguide.com offers a list of Web sites with salary information. Other Web sites that provide compensation data are salary.com, jobsmart.org, salarycompensation.net, salarysource.com, salaryexpert.com, and wageweb.com. Many Internet employment sites such as careerbuilders.com and monster.com also offer some salary information. In addition, salaries listed for job postings on employment sites and in newspapers will give you a feel for the market. Salary surveys can also help you determine the market value of any particular position. Although most salary survey Web sites charge an access fee, wageweb.com provides free access to national salary information for more than 160 benchmark positions in the following fields: finance, engineering, sales and marketing, administration, health care, manufacturing, and information technology. For a fee, you can also view salary data from their 1500 member organizations categorized by geography, size of organization or industry. Valuable salary information is also available from trade and professional organizations in your field. Even if an organization does not directly compile the data you are seeking, you may be able to obtain helpful information by talking to members who work in your field. Yahoo.com provides a listing of business and professional organizations in its commercial directory at www.yahoo.com/business_and_economy/organizations/professional/. Moreover, women's professional organizations or women's groups within professional organizations such as the Financial Women's Association, Business and Professional Women, 9 to 5 National Association of Working Women, the National Association for Female Executives, or the Association of Women in Real Estate may be helpful.

Employees or ex-employees are an excellent resource for researching the salary structure of a particular company. Current employees can provide you with up-to-date information on salaries and benefits, as well as the types of salary increases that have been given over the last few years. Although information from former employees may be dated, it is still valuable, and their greater willingness to talk about sensitive issues such as compensation makes it worth your while to seek them out. You will be surprised how many of your friends and relatives know employees and ex-employees of various companies. All you have to do is ask.

When you change jobs or ask for a raise, information about what other companies are paying for similar positions will help you highlight the value of your job. This information is especially important for women because, on average, they still earn less than men in similar positions. The market value, not your current salary, should be the basis for salary discussions. If you must disclose your current salary, or if you are in discussions with your current employer, make it clear that you know that you are being underpaid. Without being defensive or accusatory, be prepared to explain why that has occurred and to offer specifics about what other companies are paying for individuals with your skills. For example, you might state, "Companies are paying between $80,000 and $100,000 for graphic designers. Although I have only been earning $65,000 while I have been learning CAD technology, now that I am fully proficient, I expect to be paid market rates."

DISCUSSING YOUR CURRENT COMPENSATION

A candidate's current compensation is usually the single most important factor in an employer's decision as to how much to offer. Therefore, it is to your benefit to disclose as little about your compensation as possible. Most employers will try to find out exactly what you are earning and offer just enough more to make it worth your while to change jobs. For a position at the same level, that usually involves a 10 to 15 percent increase. If the new position involves a promotion, the increase will normally be larger. In addition, if the job requires relocation to a higher-cost area, the employer will typically add a differential to cover any increase in the cost of living. However, if prospective employers do not know what you are currently earning, they cannot use that information to develop their offer. As a result they will have to base their offer on what they think the market is for someone with your skills and experience.

Avoiding the topic, or, if you cannot, being as vague as possible about your current compensation, can make a world of difference in the salary you are offered. In my previous book, *Get More Money on Your Next Job,* I have a whole chapter on how to do this tactfully. Try to avoid the topic until you actually receive an offer. If you are asked about your compensation, say something like, "It's too early in the process to talk about compensation," or, "Let's talk about the job. If it's the right job for me and I'm the right person for the job, salary won't be an issue." Never tell prospective employers what it will take to hire you. If you do, you will usually get what you ask for, and it will probably be less than they were prepared to pay you. Let them make an offer. If they ask you what you are looking for in compensation, you might respond by asking them "what do you have budgeted for the position?" or give a vague answer, such as, "It depends. I want to look at the total package. What did you have in mind?"

Remember, when potential employers interview you, they are trying to recruit you. They will be just as uncomfortable pressing you for specifics about your current compensation as you are in trying to avoid the topic. If you are polite but firm, they will usually let it drop. A statement such as, "I really don't feel comfortable talking about compensation in more detail until you're sure you want to extend me an offer" will often put off the discussion until they are ready to make you an offer. At that point, you can just ask them to give you their best offer. This approach will not work with search firms. They will insist on more specific information about your compensation to be sure that they do not waste a lot of time on a candidate who, in the end, might want more money than the company is willing to pay.

The key to dealing with questions about your current salary or what you are looking for is to prepare your answers in advance. You know that these issues will come up, so be prepared with your answers. When you cannot avoid the discussion, your goal should be to create uncertainty about what it will take to get you to accept the position and, as discussed in Chapter 3, to anchor the discussion at as high a level as possible.

Talk about your total compensation, not just base salary. Use an approximation, such as, "My total compensation is in the low six figures." Include your bonus, stock, perks, and any other benefits in valuing your total compensation. Value, and describe, those items as favorably as possible without being dishonest. For example, if the bonus you earned last year was significantly larger than what you anticipate receiving this year, state your compensation in terms of what you earned last year. If, on the other hand, you expect to receive a larger bonus this year, talk about what you expect to receive in total compensation this year. If your compensation has varied significantly from year to year due to bonuses, commissions or stock options, you can talk about "earning as much as" whatever the highest figure was. You can also talk in terms of earning potential. For example, you might say "I could earn X dollars if we hit our bonus targets," or, if you are having a good year, you could state "I expect to earn X dollars this year, including bonus and stock awards." If you have a raise due shortly, include it when you describe your current compensation. Thus, you might say, "I expect to receive a salary of at least X dollars when I receive my performance review next month." People frequently make the mistake of failing to take into consideration an impending raise or bonus when they are negotiating a new position. A 10 percent salary increase in a new job does not look nearly so enticing if you are about to receive a 5 percent raise in your current job.

HOW YOU ASK MATTERS

People almost never lose a job offer because of *what* they ask for. When they do, it usually is because of *how* they ask for it. If you provide reasons to justify your requests, you may not get everything you want, but you will usually get something, and you will also gain respect for how you go about asking. Treat compensation discussions as a collaborative effort. You might say, "Here are the problems with the offer. What can we do to overcome them?" or "I have another offer, but I really want to work here. Is there any way you could make your offer more competitive?" You do not want to come across as strident but you need to be firm about your expectations. Never threaten or make "demands." This is particularly important for women, because they are held to a different standard than men and are usually expected to adopt a more relational negotiating style.

BE ENTHUSIASTIC ABOUT THE JOB

Whether you are dealing with a new employer or seeking a raise from your current employer, you want to let them know that you really like the company and the job. It also doesn't hurt to let your boss or prospective boss know how much you want to work with him or her. Enthusiasm is the single most important quality employers seek in their employees. Being enthusiastic will help you stand out from every other candidate for the job. Managers want employees who want to work for their company, who want to work for them, and who are going to come to work each day excited about what they are doing. So be sure to let prospective employers know—repeatedly—how excited you are about the job opportunity. You do not want to leave any uncertainty in their minds about how much you want the job, only how much they will have to pay to get you to accept their offer. Similarly, when seeking a raise from your current employer, emphasize that you love your job. At the same time, however, whenever you discuss compensation, make it clear that even though you want the job, or want to continue working in your current company, it has to make sense financially. Then work with the employer to improve the offer so that it does.

IT'S NOT ONLY ABOUT THE MONEY

We are not talking just about negotiating, or not negotiating, for more money. In fact, negotiating about other things besides money can sometimes have an even greater impact on your professional success. Frequently, when men accept new positions, they will seek, and get, commitments for the resources that they believe are necessary for them to succeed in the job. Women typically fail to do so. Many women have been brought up to believe that if they do a good job, they will be given the resources they need and will be rewarded for their efforts. While that may be true in lower-level administrative positions, it is not always true as one moves up the corporate ladder. It's much easier to get commitments for resources such as additional staff, an increased budget, a larger expense account, or additional training before you accept a position. Once you are in the job, you will be competing with many others for your share of the available resources. Getting a commitment in advance for what you need can often mean the difference between success and failure.

If you are a member of a union or work for the government, your salary may be governed by a set pay scale. Your vacation and certain other benefits may be governed by seniority. You may not think that there is anything to negotiate, yet opportunities do exist. Sometimes you can negotiate where you are placed on the salary scale based on prior experience. You may also be able to use your experience to negotiate a higher-level position that will place you on a different salary schedule. Many women succeed in negotiating a more flexible work schedule. If you are a teacher, you might be able to negotiate which classes you will teach. You can also try to negotiate about issues that may not covered by the labor agreement, such as training opportunities. Prepare for this discussion by talking with current and former employees to find out what special arrangements employees have negotiated in the past.

BE CAREFUL ABOUT HAVING SOMEONE NEGOTIATE FOR YOU

Remember that the people with whom you are negotiating your compensation will be your colleagues once you join the company. Your ultimate success will depend on how well you develop these relationships over time. So you should seek to protect these relationships right from the start. CNN anchor Jan Hopkins suggests that one way to do that is to have someone negotiate for you. Jan works in an industry in which having an agent or lawyer negotiate the terms of your employment is common. This is not true for most people outside the entertainment industry, except for senior executives. It is not only impractical, but for most people having a lawyer negotiate for them actually works against them. When you let someone else negotiate on your behalf, you lose a major advantage: the ability to use your relationship with your boss or your prospective boss.

Employment negotiations are different from other negotiations, particularly when you are talking to a new employer. The company is trying to recruit you. They want you to accept their offer, and they want you to feel good about it. For you, this is a very favorable negotiating paradigm. The minute you bring in a third party, though, you lose that advantage. Then it becomes a "negotiation." That is why we recommend you do the negotiating yourself, and, to the extent possible, do it directly with your future boss. He or she has the most at stake in hiring you. Take advantage of that and make them your ally in the negotiating process. If you do that, they will work hard to make sure that you are happy with the company's offer.

Lawyers and accountants play a useful role in employment negotiations as advisers. They can help you develop a negotiating strategy, assist you in anticipating problems, and show you how to avoid them. However, in most instances, using a lawyer or another third party to negotiate directly on your behalf changes how the other side views the process. Instead of looking for ways to entice you to join the company, the process becomes a zero-sum salary negotiation. The company brings in its lawyer, and the negotiation turns into attempts by the lawyers to show their clients that they are earning their fee or salary. If you do decide to use a third party to negotiate your salary, it is generally best do so only after you have already negotiated as much of the package as possible yourself.

Understanding the intricacies of how to use a third party effectively helped a client of mine negotiate an employment package well beyond anything she initially thought was possible. My client was a female executive who was an excellent negotiator except when it came to negotiating for herself. She had spent most of her career at one company and had risen from being a secretary to running a major business there. As she progressed within the company, her salary did not keep pace with the added responsibility she assumed. Because she had started at such a low salary, her compensation remained well below market, even with good raises and periodic salary adjustments. When someone she knew at another company asked her if she would be interested in helping them start a similar business, she came to me for advice. She asked me to negotiate for her. I told her I would be happy to help her but suggested that she negotiate with the president of the company herself. She was not comfortable doing that. However, because the new company was located in another city, we created an alternative negotiating approach that worked for her. I prepared her to meet with her prospective boss in person. She agreed to listen to his offer and discuss anything she felt comfortable addressing. At the end of that discussion, she would thank him and tell him she was very excited about the opportunity but that there were some issues she wanted to think about and would get back to him. The follow-up discussion of those issues took place by phone, with me sitting right next to her, and passing her notes any time she needed help, but without her future boss aware that I was even involved. By approaching the negotiation in this way, she had the best of both worlds: She allowed her future boss to "recruit" her, but she had me there to advise her and to help her maintain her resolve on the important issues.

It is just as important to be creative about the *substance* of what you negotiate as it is to be creative about the *way* you negotiate it. How you position something or what you call something can make all the difference in the world. When Hearst Magazines President Cathleen Black was being recruited to be President of *USA Today,* she knew that there were some significant risks in accepting the job. So she told the chairman that she would accept the position only if she were given a contract. He refused because "none of the company's executives have contracts." So she talked to a lawyer and determined what protections she felt she needed. Instead of introducing her lawyer into the process and seeking a formal contract, she got the chairman to agree to guarantee her certain things in writing. Those written guarantees were just as legally enforceable as a formal contract and provided her with the same protection. Because she did not call it a contract, though, it took the heat out of the discussion. In that way, she was able to achieve her objectives without forcing the company to abandon its practice of not giving its executives "contracts."

AN AUCTION IS A TYPE OF NEGOTIATION: TAKING ADVANTAGE OF ANOTHER OFFER

When you are negotiating with a prospective employer, it helps to have another offer to use as leverage. A second offer, properly used, creates an environment similar to an auction. If you have ever attended an auction, you know that when more than one person wants something, people tend to be willing to pay more than they would otherwise. The psychology that underlies an auction encourages this phenomenon. The fact that someone else is willing to pay more for an item leads you to question how you initially valued it. Moreover, because bids are increased in small increments, you find it much easier to rationalize paying more. Each time you increase your bid, you are adjusting your valuation from a new and higher anchor. Also, the psychological importance that individuals with a competitive negotiating style place on winning leads them to be willing to pay more. Finally, the need to make a decision quickly, before someone else prevails, creates a fear that, if you do not act immediately, you will lose an opportunity that may not become available to you again. This is akin to the psychology stores use when they hold one-day sales.

Having another offer creates an extremely favorable negotiating environment. A second offer eliminates current salary from the equation and increases feelings of self-worth and confidence. You do not feel that you "owe" a duty to either company. Moreover, you do not even have to actively negotiate; all you have to do is effectively manage the process. What most people don't recognize is that they have the power to create this "auction" environment. When you do, you create a new negotiating paradigm—one that will enable you to earn what you are really worth, regardless of what you are presently earning.

One way to use two competing opportunities is to negotiate with both at the same time and simply accept the best offer. To do that, you need only to let them both know that you are talking with someone else, without diminishing your enthusiasm for the opportunity each is offering you. A statement such as, "I am really excited about the possibility of working here, but I wanted you to know that I am also talking to another company that is interested in me," can be very effective.

All things being equal, if two companies are trying to recruit you, it would seem to make sense to simply accept the best offer. In real life, however, all things are rarely equal. You're likely to have a preference. Which company you prefer may have nothing to do with compensation. You may like one boss more than the other. One company may be offering you benefits that the other cannot: more opportunity, better job security, or special training, for example. If you have a preference, the best way to take advantage of a second offer is use it to get the company you prefer to improve its offer. Once you have an offer from each, begin with the company you like less and negotiate a better offer. Because the primary purpose of this offer is as leverage, you will be able to push hard to improve it. Once you have gotten as much as you can from the first company, you can go to your future boss and truthfully say: "I have this very generous offer from another company, but, the truth is, I'd much rather work for you. I can't just ignore the difference in what they're offering, but if you could put together a package that's in the same ball-park, I would start tomorrow."

To create an auction environment, you do not even have to actually have another offer. You can often improve your bargaining position simply by talking to another employer at the same time that you are negotiating an offer. Just having other *possibilities* will give you the confidence to insist on getting what you are worth. It will also give you the courage to walk away if you do not get it. Moreover, the fact that someone else may enter into the bidding will put pressure on the company to complete the negotiations quickly and to make you the best possible offer. You can inform the company of those discussions by stating something like, "Although you are clearly my first choice, I want you to know that I am also talking with X company, and I didn't want you to hear that on the street." This approach will work even if you have initiated the discussions with the second company and even if there is no actual job currently available. Your prospective employer will not know the exact nature of your discussions but only that another company is interested.

GETTING THE PROMOTION OR RAISE YOU DESERVE

Asking for a raise is different from negotiating with a new employer. Unfortunately, the way the process normally works disadvantages women. As discussed earlier, raises tend to be calculated as a percentage of a person's base salary. Because women often start off being paid less than men, the actual amounts of their raises tend to be smaller even when the percentage increases are the same. The effects of this disparity are compounded over time. It is a lot easier to negotiate a large salary increase when you are changing employers than to do so with your current employer. A new employer does not know your current salary unless you tell them and must therefore look to the market to determine what to offer. By contrast, nonpromotional raises are often constrained by company guidelines that set a maximum amount for a position, usually expressed as a percentage of a base salary. This means that loyalty to a single company, which should be rewarded, often tends to keep salaries low.

Men and women view discussions with other companies about employment opportunities differently. Many women consider it an act of disloyalty to talk with other employers and do so only when dissatisfied with their current position. Men, on the other hand, treat discussions with other employers as a way to test the market and do it routinely. This has major implications in terms of salary, because one of the best negotiating tools to precipitate a large raise is an offer from another employer. For this reason, staying on top of employment opportunities is invaluable.

Using another offer with your present employer, without jeopardizing your current position, is tricky. This does raise questions of loyalty and needs to be handled carefully. Even if you have a firm offer in hand, never make your employer feel that you are presenting an ultimatum. If you do, you had better be prepared to accept the other offer, because there is a good chance that your employer will leave you no choice. Even if they don't, your employer may never fully trust you again and will always be wondering when the next ultimatum will be delivered.

Therefore, it is usually best to just let your employer know that you have received another offer, but, at the same time, make it clear that you do not intend to accept it. In that way, you avoid being perceived as presenting an ultimatum. Tell your boss, "I wanted to let you know that I've been talking with X company because I didn't want you to hear it elsewhere. I'm not going to accept their offer because I really like it here. I was speaking to them because they were offering much more money than I am currently making. I hope that, going forward, you can help get the company to bring my compensation up to market, since it is clearly well below market." This approach reaffirms your loyalty to the company and makes your boss an ally in helping to get your salary adjusted, avoiding an adversarial situation.

Judge Kathleen Roberts, a professional mediator and former U.S. Magistrate, recounts one example of a too-familiar story. A friend of hers was considering leaving government to go back into the private practice of law. She was considering returning to the firm where she previously worked and was in discussions with one of the partners. Kathleen suggested that she also talk with some other firms, but her friend wouldn't even consider doing so because she felt it would be a betrayal of trust.

This is a common example of how women allow relationships to hold them back when they negotiate compensation. No man we know would have ignored Kathleen's excellent advice. The fact that her friend had worked at the firm before, knew how it operated, and got along well with the other lawyers there increased her value to the firm. Yet instead of using her relationship there to improve her bargaining position, she allowed it to hold her back. This woman would certainly have been able to negotiate a higher salary if she had competing offers from other firms. Under the circumstances, she could have been very open about the fact that, even though she really wanted to return to her old firm, she owed it to herself to talk to other firms as well. Testing the market is part of what you do when you prepare to negotiate salary. No one at her old firm would have held it against her. They would, however, have offered her more money to make sure she returned to work for them.

Too often, women allow their relationships with their employers to keep them from asking for the salary they could otherwise command. Men tend to treat their employment as just another business deal, whereas women focus on their relationships with bosses and coworkers. In the end, this can work against you. For example, suppose you go to your boss to ask for a raise. He or she responds that it is a bad time to discuss a raise because business is slow. Most men would not accept that response. Men will review their options and raise the issue again at a more opportune moment, perhaps after another employer has expressed interest. Many women will simply let the matter drop, out of fear that pressing it will damage their relationship with the boss. That does not necessarily have to be the case. It depends on your approach. You could explore your alternatives and bring the matter up again later. You could talk about a time frame for a future raise by saying, for example, "Can we agree, then, that when business picks up you will give me a 10 percent raise?" Or you could ask to revisit the issue in a month and see where things stand at that time. The main point is: you do not have to give up a raise that you deserve just to avoid the discomfort of disagreeing with someone with whom you have a relationship.

Knowing your options is just as important when you are seeking a raise from your current employer as when you are changing jobs. Even if you are happy in your current position, you should periodically test the job market, particularly if someone, either a recruiter or an employer, approaches you. This situation is not about loyalty; it is about value. Human nature is such that we tend to undervalue the familiar in favor of the new and different. We also tend to value what other people value. As a result, companies take their longtime employees for granted, particularly if it appears that these employees are unlikely to leave. If you want to be paid what you are worth, never allow employers to take you for granted. Let them know if another company approaches you, even if you do not directly use the opportunity to negotiate a raise. This reinforces the idea that you are a talented and sought-after individual.

The following tips will help you get your current employer to pay you what you are worth:

It Is Not Enough to Just Do Good Work; People Need to Know About Your Accomplishments

You should constantly market yourself internally, not just at review time, but all year long. Make sure that your boss and other key people in the company know what you are doing. Build a case throughout the year for increasing your salary. Keep a record of your achievements and get them in front of your boss a few months before you are actually scheduled for your annual review. If you wait until right before the review, not only will this look obvious, but also the decisions will probably already have been made. Send copies of relevant memos to your boss and other key individuals. Share credit for your successes with your boss and your subordinates. In fact, one way to inform key people of your accomplishments is to commend your subordinates for their work on projects you are responsible for.

Make Your Boss's Priorities Your Priorities

The better you make your boss look to his or her superiors and peers, the more valuable you will be and the harder your boss will work to make sure you are happy with your compensation. Instead of letting your relationship with your boss become a disadvantage, use it to advance your cause. If you are being paid below market, marshall the facts and take advantage of that relationship. Ask your boss for advice and help in rectifying the situation.

Accept Additional Responsibilities and Make Your Interest in Being Promoted Known

There is no such thing as a free lunch. This is as true in business as it is in life. Salary increases usually bring with them more work and responsibility. So learn new skills and seek additional responsibilities whenever you can, even if you are not in a position to get a raise or a promotion immediately. After you have shown you can do the job, then ask for the raise or promotion. Often the deciding factor in who gets a promotion is who wants it most. So let your boss know you are interested in being promoted. One of the best ways to do that is to ask for advice and help. When you ask your boss "What must I do to get promoted?" you are in effect asking for both. If you follow the advice you receive and check periodically to see how you are coming along, your boss will normally do everything possible to see that you get the promotion you are seeking.

Jerri DeVard, Chief Marketing Officer for Citibank's eConsumer Group, describes how she used this approach to get a promotion when she was Vice President for Marketing at Pillsbury. At the time, sales and marketing were separate departments. She felt that, for business reasons, it made sense to combine sales and marketing into one department. So, as she went about trying to demonstrate that it would be more effective to combine them, she began working more closely with the sales department and so did her staff. By the time she actually went to her boss to suggest that the two departments be merged into one, the decision was easy because the departments were already working so closely together. And she was promoted to Vice President of Sales and Marketing to head the combined department.

Periodically Test Your Market Value

In most cases, the approaches discussed above will help you to enable your employer to increase your compensation. However, if you are well below market, some employers will feel constrained as to how much they feel they can increase your salary. They are concerned that if they give you a raise that significantly exceeds their guidelines, they will have to do the same for others. In that case, you may have to use another offer, as discussed above, to convince your employer to raise your salary sufficiently.

It is useful for your boss to know that from time to time you are approached by other employers. You can take the initiative to ensure that happens. Develop relationships with recruiters in your industry. Be helpful to them when they call, even if you are not interested in the position they are filling. Become active in professional organizations.

If all else fails, you have to be prepared to walk away and accept a position with another company. Your willingness and ability to do so will enable you to negotiate more confidently with your present employer. The same basic concepts apply whether you are asking for a raise or negotiating with a new employer. Know your worth, ask for what you want, and be willing to walk away if you don't get it.

10

Buying or Leasing a Car

Be Prepared for Traditional Negotiating Tactics, or Change the Way You Negotiate

When KPMG executive Terri Santisi went to a local automobile dealership to lease a Land Rover, she knew exactly what she wanted and, based on her research, approximately what it should cost. Eventually a salesman came up to her. She gave him her business card, so he knew she was a senior executive with one of the largest consulting firms in the country. She told him exactly what car she wanted and with what options. She also let him know that she was prepared to lease the car that day. Then she asked about price. He said he needed to "run some numbers" and went into another room. When he returned, he gave her a lease price that was well above anything her research indicated would have been reasonable and much more than she was pay-ing for her current Land Rover with similar options. She told him that the numbers didn't make sense and proceeded to explain why: "Interest rates were lower. The dollar was stronger than when she had leased her last Land Rover. That should have resulted in lower prices, even considering price increases since the last time she leased a car." Certainly there was no way he could justify the price quoted to her. The salesman responded, "Miss, what Alan Greenspan does with interest rates has no impact on lease payments or car loans." She thought to herself, "This person can't just have said that to me." What do you say when your intelligence has just been insulted? So she got up and walked out. She waited two weeks, and then had her husband call the same dealer. She showed her husband all her research and told him approximately what he should be able to get. She listened in on the other line when he called, and he was able to negotiate the lease price Terri had suggested, which was signifi-cantly lower than what the first salesman had offered her.

As frustrating as this experience was for her, Terri responded like the excellent negotiator she is. There was no way that she could convince that salesperson to give her a good price, so she got someone else to deliver the message. She could have leased the car somewhere else, but the dealer was convenient, she had received good service in the past, and they had the car she wanted. Terri didn't take it personally nor try to enlighten the salesman. She simply selected the right person to negotiate the deal.

Unfortunately, Terri's experience is not unique. Several of the women we interviewed described buying or leasing cars as among their worst negotiating experiences. Executive recruiter Pat Mastandrea, who has negotiated successfully with the likes of Barry Diller, Chairman of USA Networks, and Rupert Murdoch, Chairman of News Corp., experienced similar treatment the last time she leased a car. Her response illustrates how to create something different when the negotiating model you face does not suit you.

The lease on her Pathfinder was almost up. Pat liked the car, so she went back to the dealer where she had leased it. She wanted to simply roll over the lease and get a new Pathfinder. The first thing the salesperson did was tell her that, because her lease had two months remaining on it, she would have to pay a fee to get out of it early. She responded by telling him: "In that case, I will come back in two months." He quickly reconsidered and told her that he would take care of it. Then he proceeded to negotiate with her. After they reached an agreement, he went into another room for a few minutes. When he came back, he told her that his manager would not approve the deal and began to try to renegotiate a higher payment. Pat walked out.

She considered what other options were available and decided to negotiate differently by buying a car over the Internet—not because she couldn't negotiate with the dealer, but because she did not want to. She went to carsdirect.com and found the car she wanted, with the options she wanted, in the color she wanted, for a few thousand dollars less than her local dealer had quoted her. According to Pat, "When a woman walks into a regular dealership, they assume she is easy. There is always a shortage of the car you want, they are not sure if they can get it for you in the color you want, and you will probably have to pay over list." When she leased a car over the Internet, no one told her what they couldn't do. They just found the car she wanted at a reasonable price.

Not every dealership treats women badly. Kitty Van Bortel built one of the largest Subaru dealerships in the country with annual sales in excess of $45 million by catering to women. She believes most dealers "do not understand women and do not treat them well." She has sought to run her dealership differently.

Kitty started selling used cars part-time while she was in college. After college, she sold Fords and then Mercedes at dealers where she was the only female salesperson. She was a top producer and became the first and only female sales manager the Mercedes dealer ever had. As a salesperson, she watched how the salesmen treated women who came in alone. At first they ignored them because they didn't want to waste their time with them. Most of the salesmen believed that women could not make a decision without speaking to their husband, father, or boyfriend. Kitty made an excellent living taking advantage of the fact that the male sales staff did not want to sell to women.

She also realized there was a tremendous opportunity for someone willing to change the way women bought cars. The idea came to her one night when she was watching Larry King do a live broadcast from the Detroit Auto Show. He was interviewing the CEOs from what were then known as the Big Three auto companies, Ford, General Motors, and Chrysler. A woman viewer called in and said, "I do not understand why I have to fight to get a good price when I go into a dealership." One of the CEOs replied, "The reason is that most people like to negotiate. It's fun. And you are the exception." When the other two CEOs agreed, Kitty decided these men just did not understand women. So she set out to open a dealership that marketed specifically to women.

Kitty's Subaru dealership offers a different way of buying a car, with an eye to making women feel comfortable. For one thing, 75 percent of her sales staff are women. Unlike typical dealerships, which pay their salespeople a commission based on the purchase price of the car, thereby encouraging them to pressure customers into buying things they do not need or want, her salespeople receive a flat fee for every car sold. There is no pressure or haggling over price. Prices are fixed and posted. Kitty seeks to make a fair profit, but the customers know that they are getting a good price. She also understands that many women feel more comfortable taking their time when making such a major decision, so her salespeople encourage them to go home and think about it.

While you might find the car buying experience Kitty offers appealing, you may not want to travel to Rochester, New York, or to buy a Subaru. So we asked Kitty how women can negotiate more effectively with local car dealers. Here is her advice:

RESEARCH THE DEALER'S COST

Before you go to buy, figure out which car you want, and with what options. Test-drive the car. If you find more than one car with which you would be happy, you will be able to negotiate a better deal. But, in that case, you will have to do your homework with regard to each model. Once you have decided on a car, log on to one or more of the free Internet sites that you can use to get information: kbb.com, edmunds.com, and carprice.com are just a few. In addition, for an annual fee, you can join consumerreports.org, which gives not only price information but also information about performance and safety.

Your Internet research will tell you almost exactly what the dealer paid for the model you want to buy, including any rebates from the manufacturer. To determine what the dealer paid for the car, add the base invoice price, the invoice price for any options you select, and destination charges, then subtract from that figure any special factory incentives or year-end rebates available to the dealer. Dealers also get what is known as a "holdback" of between 2 and 4 percent from the car manufacturer. The holdback was originally intended to offset the dealer's cost of keeping cars on the lot but is now just a rebate to the dealers. The holdback is the same whether a dealer sells the car on the day it is delivered or it sits on the lot for months. The Web sites listed above provide holdbacks for specific cars. In addition, manufacturers offer special rebates, sometimes referred to as "factory" or "year-end" incentives at different times of the year and for models that are not selling well. Dealers sometimes pass on these rebates directly to the consumer in the form of "dealer cash back" specials or below-market interest rates.

MAKE THE DEALER AN OFFER

After you determine what the dealer paid for the car you want, you are ready to buy. You can get most American cars for $200 over the dealer's cost. Dealers are willing to do this because with the manufacturer's holdback, they still make a fair profit. Sometimes, at the end of the month or at the end of the model year, dealers are willing to sell cars at cost. However, if you want a hot-selling model that is in short supply, you may have to pay a premium greater than $200. You may also have to pay more than $200 over dealer's cost for certain Japanese or European cars. Most Internet sites that offer price data will also have information on how much over invoice different types of automobiles have recently sold for. For example, edmunds.com provides information it calls "true market value," which reflects what different cars are actually selling for in various parts of the country. This information is particularly useful when determining what to pay for hot-selling cars that are commanding premium prices.

When you know what you should be paying for the car you want, go to the showroom and tell the salesperson that you have done your homework. Then tell the salesperson what you are willing to pay. You need to create the negotiating paradigm. The key to successfully negotiating the price of a new car is to anchor the discussions from the dealer's cost, never from the manufacturer's suggested retail price (MSRP), the sticker price on the car window. Do not accept the negotiating model that salespeople will try to use. Where you allow the negotiations to start will determine where you cnd up. Never negotiate down from the sticker price. Ignore the sticker price. Negotiate up from the dealer's cost. Be prepared to walk away and go someplace else if salespeople won't meet your price. Although Kitty recommends offering $200 over the dealer's costs and walking away if the salesperson doesn't agree, we suggest that you offer to buy the car at cost and then let them convince you that they need to make a profit. You will still end up at $200 over cost, or at whatever is a reasonable markup for the type of car you are buying, but the salesperson will feel as if he or she has gotten something.

Dealers will try to sell you an extended warranty and credit life insurance. Extended warranties are seldom a good value when you consider the manufacturer's warranty that comes with the car. Credit life insurance is usually an even worse value. If you need more life insurance, you can almost always get it more cheaply from an insurance company. Finally, you should not have to pay for document handling, other than perhaps a nominal charge of no more than $50, or for any other additional dealer fees. The only fees you should be paying are destination charges, state sales tax, and the license and registration fees actually charged by your state.

If you decide to buy a used car, the same basic negotiating approaches work. The only variable is that used cars, even of the same make, model, and year, can vary significantly in condition. Be sure to have someone you trust—your regular mechanic, for example—inspect the car before you purchase it, whether you are buying from an individual or a dealer. The warranties offered by the dealer as well as the dealer's reputation are also important.

Car dealers are particularly motivated to move their inventory at certain times, for example, the end of the month when they need to make room for new cars being delivered. At those times, they may give you a better price or throw in extras such as free oil changes for a year. At the end of the model year, dealers often sell cars at or below cost because after the new models arrive, they can no longer sell last year's models at this year's prices. Often manufacturers provide dealers with year-end rebates of up to 5 percent, which can be used to negotiate a lower purchase price.

Keep in mind that most salespeople get paid on commission. The more you pay for your car, the more they earn. They also may get a bonus for selling you an extended warranty or other dealer options such as fabric treatment or rustproofing. Although salespeople want to sell you the car for as high a price as possible, making the sale is even more important. If you walk away and do not buy the car, they will not get paid anything.

Once armed with the dealer's cost information, you also have the option of going in and haggling. If you choose to do that, determine the price you are willing to pay, be prepared to say "no," and, most importantly, be prepared to walk away, because you will probably have to do so at least once. We would also suggest that you bring a friend along for moral support.

Golf course executive Cathy Harbin's most recent experience helping a friend lease a car is an example of that type of negotiating. Cathy and her friend went to a local dealer. The friend described the make and model of the car she wanted to lease, the basic options, and how much she was willing to put down as a down-payment. Then she asked what the monthly payments would be for their best deal, and specified actual payments including everything, no extras. The salesman quoted her $350 per month. She thanked the salesman and told him, "That was way too much and that they would just keep looking." As they got up to leave, the salesman said, "Wait a minute. How much do you want to pay?" Cathy responded, "Just tell me the best you can do." After going back and forth for a while trying to get Cathy to make an offer, he finally said, "Well, let me go ask my manager." He then came back with an offer of $320 a month." Cathy asked if that included keyless entry, pinstriping, and a CD player. He informed her that those features were not included at that price. Cathy replied that they were in no rush. Her friend's car was fine for now, she said, and they could keep looking until they found one at the price they wanted. The salesman asked what that price was, and Cathy eventually told him that they would not pay more than $300 a month. He balked, and, after more haggling, he finally offered $307. Cathy said no, and prepared to leave. The salesman asked, "Are you really going to walk away for $7?" Without missing a beat, she responded, "Are you really going to let us walk away for $7?" Then they left. The salesman called Cathy at home that afternoon. They agreed to split the difference and her friend ended up paying $303.50.

Few women enjoy this type of bargaining. We include it here to illustrate not only how to haggle, a skill you sometimes need in order to avoid being taken advantage of, but, more important, to illustrate how Cathy deals with being underestimated because she is a woman. The salesman started the negotiations with a very high offer, probably because he was dealing with two women. Cathy did not let that upset her. She just kept being herself and remained firm in her position until she got the price she wanted. This is good advice in any negotiation.

TRADING IN YOUR OLD CAR

Another way dealers make money is by buying your old car and then reselling it. This is seldom a win-win negotiation because the less they pay for your car, the more they make when they sell it. Be careful when trading in your old car. What you gain by negotiating a good price for a new car can easily be lost when you negotiate the price for your trade-in. Dealers can offer a relatively high price for a trade-in by inflating the sales price of the new car you are purchasing. Although this might look like a good deal, you will end up paying more than you would if you negotiated your best price for a new car and accepted the "blue-book" value on your trade. You can avoid this by negotiating the purchase price for the new car before you discuss a trade-in. If the salesperson asks about a trade-in before you have agreed on a purchase price, simply say you have not decided what you want to do with your old car.

The Internet also offers a wealth of information that will enable you to determine the value of your trade-in. The same Web sites that provide cost information on new cars also provide information on buying and selling used cars. Expect to get the wholesale price for your trade-in. That is the blue-book price, or the price the dealer could get by selling it to a used car dealer the next day, not the price for similar cars being advertised in the newspaper or on the Internet. You cannot expect to get a wholesale price from the dealer when you purchase a new car and, at the same time, get a retail price from the dealer on your trade-in. Therefore you might consider selling your old car yourself. Although you will receive a slight savings in terms of a lower sales tax on the net purchase price if you trade in your old car to the dealer, that may be more than offset by the greater amount you could get if you were willing to sell it yourself. Be sure, however, if you decide to sell your used car by advertising in the newspaper or online that you take adequate precautions to ensure your own personal safety.

FINANCING YOUR PURCHASE

Dealers can also increase their profit when they negotiate financing on a new or used car. Be careful about how you finance the car. Check the interest rates being offered through local banks and over the Internet before you go to the showroom. Frequently, though, you can get a good deal financing through the dealer, and, at certain times of the year, automobile manufacturers offer below-market-rate promotions to increase sales. Be aware that local dealers are allowed to add up to several percentage points, known as a dealer markup, to whatever interest rate their national lender establishes for customers, based on their income and the credit history the dealer obtains by running a credit check while you are arranging the financing. If you have not done your homework, some dealers may try to take advantage by adding a dealer markup to the financing rate they quote to you. Anti-discrimination lawsuits have been filed against the financing arms of several car manufacturers claiming that they use the dealer markup to charge higher rates to minorities. Some dealers may do the same when negotiating with women. You can protect yourself by researching your financing options ahead of time.

LEASING A CAR

You can use a mathematical formula to determine what it should cost to lease a car, based on the purchase price. Several computer programs are available that take the purchase price and convert it into a monthly lease rate depending on your down payment, the length of the lease, and prevailing interest rates. One such program can be purchased at leasewizard.com. As part of your preparation, you can use dealer cost data to determine approximately how much you should end up paying in monthly lease payments while varying options such as the length of the lease and the amount of the down payment. This allows you to approach the transaction as if you were buying a car. Tell the dealer that you are interested in buying a car and, using the techniques described above, negotiate the best deal you can, including your trade-in and the financing rate. Then ask what that price would convert into if you decided to lease instead. Be sure that the monthly lease payment is converted accurately, because it is hard to tell if it is wrong. Ask to see the calculations. Because of all the variables involved, it is more difficult to determine if you are getting a good deal if you negotiate the monthly lease payments directly rather than converting from a negotiated purchase price. If you do negotiate a lease directly, obtain offers from several dealers and/or Internet sites for the car and options you want, then look for the best price. Be sure that the prices quoted are based on the same length of lease and down payment.

Buying a car is no different from any other type of negotiation. The key to success is preparation, confidence, and a willingness to walk away. Unfortunately, dealers take advantage of buyers who don't understand the process. Many dealers treat women differently than they do men. In one study published in the *Harvard Law Review,* men and women went to the same dealers on different days to purchase identical cars. The initial price offered to men was significantly lower than the initial price offered to women. That difference remained even after both the men and the women negotiated the best deal they could (Ayers, "Fair Driving: Gender And Race Discrimination in Retail Car Negotiations," *Harvard Law Review,* 104, 817–872, 1991.) By following the advice set forth in this chapter, you can buy a car from your local dealer and get a fair price. Alternatively, you can change the negotiating model. You can go to a dealership like Kitty's—and there are a few—where the prices are posted and are not negotiated, or you can shop on the Internet and avoid the pressure of a showroom. Or, like Terri, you can have someone else negotiate on your behalf. What you don't have to do is pay too much for a car just because you're a woman.

11

Buying and Selling Real Estate

A Woman's Place Is in the Home—Whether You're Buying or Selling

BUYING A HOME

Preparation, vision, and creativity are the key to buying a house. Pat Mastandrea, President of The Cheyenne Group, was in the market to buy a house in Connecticut near the beach. The real estate market was red-hot, and she had already lost two houses in bidding wars. In each case, purchasers had bid up the price of the house well beyond the original asking price, and Pat had walked away.

One afternoon, her realtor called and told her about a house that was about to go on the market. The broker described it as a unique old house in a great location near the water. Pat got the floor plans for the house, did some homework, learned its history, and assured herself that it was in good shape. She knew the market, and it was clear the house would sell for at least the asking price and probably much more. Pat wanted the house, but she also wanted to avoid the hysteria that had surrounded the two other houses she had attempted to purchase. So she decided to change the negotiating paradigm and to create a new one. Before the house actually went on the market, she made an offer at the asking price, without an inspection and without any contingencies. Her only condition was that the house not be put on the market. As Pat says, "What was the worst that was going to happen?" She had seen the house recently, and she thought that, at worst, it might need a new furnace or some minor repairs. So she balanced the risk that the house might need some work against the risk of losing it and decided to change the negotiating dynamic. She ended up buying the house for approximately $500,000; five years later, it was worth over $1 million. Most of us are not in Pat's league when it comes to buying houses. We cannot afford to take the risk of buying a house without having it inspected. We can, however, take a lesson from her and approach negotiations creatively.

Have a Thorough Understanding of the Market

Your preparation begins with studying the housing market in the area you are considering. Whether the market is strong or weak, there is no substitute for knowing what you want and what similar properties are selling for in the area. For simplicity, we will just refer to buying a "house," but the same advice applies to buying a coop or a condominium. Hollywood producer, director, and writer Tamar Simon Hoffs shares some advice that she was given years ago by a Chicago real estate developer:

> Investigate the market as well as you can. Really understand the value on every level. Do not determine what you are willing to

> pay by the price tag or on an emotional basis. Figure out the
> value and base the entire negotiation on that value.

Tammy has done very well following this advice. Knowing the market is the starting point for all real estate negotiations.

When you are looking to buy a place, first familiarize yourself with the area. Research the schools, shopping, your potential commute, and the other amenities that the neighborhood has to offer. Go on the Internet, visit different areas, and select neighborhoods where you would consider living. The more flexible you are in terms of location, the more options you will have. Determine what is important to you in a house, both what you must have, and what you would like to have. Once again, the fewer your "must-haves," the more houses you will have to choose from. And the more options you have, the better your negotiating position.

Figure out what you can comfortably afford to pay, then begin to look at houses in your price range. Have a broker drive you around to look at houses. Go on the Internet to sites like realtor.com so you can get an idea of what sellers are asking for houses. Some brokers offer virtual tours of the houses they are listing. As part of your preparation, have a lender preapprove you for a mortgage, and clear up any credit problems you might have. This will make you more attractive as a buyer.

A thorough understanding of the market, including how fast houses are selling, is important. Is the market hot, or are you in a down market? In a "hot market," you must be ready to buy because good properties will not remain on the market long. When the market is hot, the key is to recognize value. If a house is fairly priced, there will not be much room to negotiate. In a hot market, or if you are dealing with a unique piece of property, the ability to act quickly can make all the difference. Your goal should be to close the deal quickly before other buyers make competing bids.

If the market is slow, on the other hand, you can afford to browse. You can negotiate about the price, ask the seller to throw in extras such as appliances, ask the seller to take back a mortgage, or just throw out a low offer to determine if there is any interest.

Put the basic negotiating principles presented throughout the book to good use. Start by making the right offer. If you offer too much, you'll pay too much. If you offer too little, you might not have the opportunity to negotiate further. So how do you know what to offer?

Find Out the Seller's Situation

In determining what to offer, start by researching "comps," recent sale prices for comparable houses. This information is a matter of public record. Ask your broker to get the comps for you, then find out what the seller's situation is. Why are the sellers moving? If a seller has to sell quickly, you are dealing with what brokers refer to as a "motivated seller" and you can usually negotiate a good deal, particularly if you are willing to close promptly. People who have been transferred, have lost their job, are getting a divorce, or have already purchased another home usually need to sell quickly. Similarly, if the owner has died, the estate will generally want to sell the house as fast as possible. On the other hand, sellers who are looking to buy a house elsewhere but do not have to move will be more likely to wait for their price. Your ability to negotiate will also be affected by how long the house has been on the market, whether there have been other offers, whether any earlier offers have fallen through, and whether the house has any special problems.

You can obtain a lot of information from your broker. As Carolyn Klemm, owner/broker at Klemm Real Estate in Litchfield, Connecticut, puts it: "Good brokers are like gossip columnists;

they know everything about everyone." It is helpful to talk directly with the sellers' broker or with the sellers themselves, if you have the opportunity. One way to do that is to ask to meet with the sellers to discuss questions you may have about the house, the schools, or the neighborhood. This gives you an opportunity to find out about the sellers' situation and to develop a relationship with them as well. Once you understand the market and the sellers' situation, you can value the property accurately and determine how to properly anchor your offer. Then make a bid.

Making some sort of bid, as long as it is reasonable, will give you information about what the seller really wants. Gina Doynow, Vice President and Manager of College Credit Card Services for Citibank, used that approach to close a deal on the apartment of her dreams. She had been looking for a two-bedroom coop within her price range, located near a park, and with a terrace and a view. She finally found what she was looking for but it needed some work. So she made a bid about 15 percent below the asking price with the aim of getting information from the broker about what the seller really wanted—more cash up-front, a speedy closing, or a higher price. As she suspected, the owner wanted a large cash down payment and a quick closing because the apartment was vacant. After she understood what the owner's interests were, she was able to structure a second offer that satisfied those interests and at the same time provided her with a good price. She got the information she needed from the broker, however, only after she made an initial bid. You can use a low bid to get information, but it must be a serious bid.

Look for What Others Don't See

When buying real estate, it helps to have vision. The market takes advantage of people who have no tolerance for renovation. Lisa

Brown, a broker at Stribling Associates who regularly sells condominiums and coops on New York's Upper East Side for millions of dollars, suggests looking for a well-priced apartment that is poorly presented. Most buyers will fail to see the potential. According to Lisa, "people who can see what other people miss" will find bargains in any type of market. Also, as Carolyn Klemm notes, "Women generally have more vision when it comes to decorating and renovating." That is a tremendous advantage when you are buying real estate. If you do not have that talent, bring someone along with you, perhaps a friend, who does. Remember, though, decorating cannot fix problems with a house. A structural inspection will reveal any major problems. Ordinarily, your offer should include a clause that allows you to cancel the deal without any penalty if an inspection reveals any significant problem. "Significant" can be defined by a dollar value in terms of the cost of remedying the problem or left to your discretion within a certain time period—for example, you can cancel without penalty within three days following the inspection. If you include an inspection clause in your offer, you then have the opportunity to renegotiate the price or get the seller to correct any major problems discovered during the inspection.

Relationships Can Work to Your Advantage

Another advantage that many women have when they negotiate is the ability to develop a relationship with the sellers' broker and the sellers themselves. Linda Gedney, a top broker for Prudential Fox and Roache, describes the importance a personal relationship can play in real estate transactions. She was working with a young couple who were trying to purchase a house just outside Philadelphia. They found a house they liked and made an offer on it, but another party also made an offer on the same house. To facilitate the negotiations, Linda wanted to get her buyers and the sellers together so they could "bond." She arranged for the couple to visit the property and asked that the sellers be there, ostensibly to answer any questions that came up. The sellers liked her clients, and, as she later found out, did not like or trust the other potential buyer, whom they knew from the neighborhood. In the end, the sellers accepted a slightly lower offer from her clients because they liked them and believed that the deal would close without any problems if they accepted their offer.

Leadership coach and former investment banker Allison Ashley, Managing Partner at Veracity International, benefited from connecting on a personal level with the broker who was handling sales for a new development. While looking at homes, she became friendly with the broker. In the course of their conversations, she let him know that she was a single mother raising two children by herself. They talked about his children, and he sympathized with how difficult it must be for her. When it came time to negotiate the price, after some discussion, Allison got him to give her what she felt was his best offer. At that point, remembering his sympathetic response to her situation, she asked, "Can't you do any better for me? I'm a single mom." Although he told her he could not lower the price any further, he agreed to lower his commission and to upgrade the carpet and tile in the house at no additional cost.

Margery Hadar, a residential real estate broker and Vice President at William B. May Co. who specializes in handling coops and condominiums on New York City's Upper East Side, shares our view that it helps to develop a relationship with the people with whom you are negotiating. It is best to try to connect directly with the sellers, but it is also useful to have a relationship with the sellers' broker. Margery believes, as we do, that it is a mistake to try to bring down the price by "knocking" the property. People, especially women, are usually proud of their homes and what they have done with them. It pays to appeal to that pride by complimenting the property rather than trying to denigrate it.

Margery tells of one deal in which a potential buyer came to her and said, "I am making what you might consider a low offer because this is the worst apartment in this building." Even though she is a professional and her only relationship with the owner was as his broker, this made her angry. She liked the apartment, and her initial reaction was, "How dare he?" In the end, she sold the apartment to someone else. Had he come in and said he loved the apartment, she would have made every effort to help him get it. Based on her years of experience selling real estate, Carolyn Klemm advises:

> If a woman comes to a home and admires it and compliments the woman of the house who is responsible for decorating it, she will be flattered. She will want to sell to someone who appreciates the house.

It is always harder to say no to someone you know, especially if you like them. So if you can get to know the sellers and their agent, it will make negotiating with them a lot easier.

Remain Emotionally Detached, and Be Willing to Walk Away

In the end, though, all your preparation, creativity, vision, and developing of relationships are no substitute for the ability to say no—to remain unemotional about the property and to be able to walk away if necessary. If you let your emotions affect how you negotiate, and buying a house can be very emotional, you will not be able to negotiate effectively. When you fall in love with a house, you cannot negotiate well because you cannot walk away. This is one of the biggest mistakes women make. Carolyn Klemm was representing Faith Stewart Gordon, the owner of the Russian Tea Room in New York City. Faith, who was looking for a place in Connecticut, found a huge converted barn. She fell in love with it and quickly went to contract on it. Once Faith had a little time to think about it, though, she realized that she had made a mistake. The house was too big, had too much land, and would cost too much to maintain. It was a great house, but it did not suit her needs. Because she was under contract, she had to go through with the purchase, but she immediately asked Carolyn to sell it for her. Luckily, Carolyn was able to resell it within a month for what Faith had paid plus her selling expenses. Although all real estate purchases are emotional, to be successful, you must be able to pull back and not negotiate emotionally.

Be Creative in Your Approach

Often the most important thing about buying or selling property is to be creative in how you approach the negotiation. When Maxine Hartley, the former President of Pearl Management and a longtime executive recruiter, was starting out as a recruiter, she worked out of a small office in a townhouse on New York's Upper East Side. Eventually she needed a larger office, but she wanted to stay in the same area. Her landlord wanted more for the additional space than she could afford, and space elsewhere in the area was exorbitant. So she took a different approach. She went to the owner of a nearby brownstone and asked him if he would allow her to gut the first floor of the building, which he was using for storage, and put in an office. She offered to hire the architect and build the office for him. In return, she wanted a 10-year lease at a below-market rent. At the end of the 10-year period, the owner would get the offices, which he could then rent out at the market rate. Everyone made out well in this deal. The owner had never thought about using the space for an office. It cost him nothing. He immediately began receiving rent from Maxine that he had not been receiving before. In addition, at the end of the lease, he had office space that he could rent out very profitably. As for Maxine, even after paying for the architect and building the office, she still got a beautiful office in a great location for less than she had been paying in rent—all because she used the *create* approach to come up with an idea about which she could negotiate.

When Tamar Simon Hoffs was looking to build a house on the beach in Malibu, she could have gone to brokers and told them what she wanted. But because there is almost no undeveloped property in Malibu, she would probably have ended up buying developed property and tearing down whatever was on it—and paying an exorbitant price as well. So, like Maxine, she took a different approach.

Tammy went to Malibu, started looking at property, and came across a beautiful piece of beachfront property that appeared to have been abandoned. She checked the town records and found out that it belonged to a local university that had received it as a gift from an alumnus. Tammy knew that the university had to be paying substantial taxes on the property, although no dormitories or classrooms could be built on it due to zoning restrictions. So she convinced the university that they would be better off selling the property than holding onto it and paying taxes in the hope that someday they might find a use for it. Eventually they agreed. Although the property was not on the market, she created a negotiating situation that was extremely favorable to her. Because the school was not in the business of selling real estate, they viewed the property differently than someone in the business might have. As a result of her creative approach, she got one of the last undeveloped pieces of Malibu beachfront property for an excellent price.

Citibank executive Jerri DeVard also had to be creative to buy an apartment in New York after moving there from New Orleans. The apartment she wanted was very expensive, but it had a number of things wrong with it. Jerri asked the owner to make some repairs or to reduce his asking price, but because the market was hot, he refused to negotiate even though he did not have another buyer. Jerri realized that she needed to change her approach. She tried to figure out what she could do to motivate him to negotiate and finally decided to look at a lower-priced apartment that was on the market in the same building. Jerri made sure, by letting his broker know, that the owner of the first apartment knew what she was doing. Once he realized that he might lose the deal, he agreed to a lower price.

It also helps to be creative with regard to other aspects of a home sale other than the price. For example, if you are not pressed to move in quickly, offer to close when it's most convenient for the sellers. That gives the sellers the feeling that they are in control. Lisa Brown points out the need for both creativity and understanding when you are buying or selling a residence. For instance, she was representing a buyer who was moving to New York. The buyer had three children starting school on September 1. She and the seller had reached an agreement on the price but could not agree on a closing date. The seller could not move into his new place until October 1 and refused to close before then. So Lisa went to him, told him about the three kids, and asked him to put himself in the position of the buyer. If he had three children moving to a new neighborhood and starting at a new school, what would he want? Then, when she offered to put him up in a hotel until he could move into his new place, he readily agreed.

SELLING YOUR HOME

Price Your Home to Sell

Knowing the market is just as critical when selling a home as when buying one. Pricing your property correctly when you initially put it on the market will determine how much you ultimately get and sometimes whether it sells at all. You typically get your best offers during the first few weeks that your house is on the market, so you want to price it to attract offers. After a house has been on the market for a period of time, people begin to wonder if there is something wrong with it. Brokers stop showing it. It becomes, as brokers say, "overexposed." One mistake that women often make is to put a house on the market at a price that cannot really be justified just to "test the market." If you are not ready to sell, do not put the house on the market. If you do, and the house does not sell, you will have difficulty selling it when you decide you really want to. Moreover, the price you ultimately receive will be lower than if you had priced it properly in the first place.

Most brokers suggest that you price a home slightly above market. If you price it too high, you will discourage potential buyers. But if you price it too low, you will not have any room to negotiate when someone makes you an offer. When William B. May Co. broker Margery Hadar represents buyers, she likes to negotiate deals in three steps: an initial offer, a second offer, and then a final offer. That way, she gets to see how the sellers react. She believes that this approach results in her getting better prices for her clients. In real estate transactions, people expect to bargain except when the market is red-hot. Whether you are dealing with buyers who use two, three, or even more steps, you should set your initial asking price at a level that is reasonable but slightly high so that you have room to bargain.

Appeal to Buyers' Emotions

As a seller, you want potential buyers to fall in love with your property. Buying a house is often an emotional decision. If a buyer becomes emotional about the property—if they can't walk away—you will be able to negotiate a better price. How a house looks and the feel you give it play a role in making that happen. Do whatever inexpensive cosmetic work is necessary to make the property look warm and inviting. A fresh coat of paint, new carpeting, and some landscaping can do wonders. Keep it neat and clean at all times so that you can show the property at a moment's notice. Clean the windows. Make sure the house smells nice, and have soothing music playing in the background when people are looking at the house. Some brokers even suggest you have bread or cookies baking in the oven. Do whatever you can to get potential buyers excited about wanting to live there.

Create Competition

As a seller, you always want to get more than one buyer interested in the property to encourage bidding competition. As discussed earlier, people want what others value. The fact that someone else is interested in the property will often result in buyers reevaluating how they originally valued the property, resulting in their offering more than they would have otherwise.

For example, William P. May Co. broker Margery Hadar was representing a couple who were selling a condominium on New York's Upper East Side in a hot market. In setting a price, they reviewed what comparable apartments had sold for in the building and in the neighborhood. Their asking price was slightly above where Margery thought the market was. She began showing the apartment early Monday morning. On the first day, they got a bid for the full asking price. Rather than accepting it, they decided to continue showing the apartment because they were afraid they had underpriced it. They told the first bidder that they wanted to keep it on the market for a week before they responded to any offers. On the second day, another buyer offered to purchase the apartment at full price. By Friday, they had a third bidder willing to pay the asking price. So Margery called all three buyers, told them that there were three offers at the asking price, and said she would be accepting sealed bids for the apartment on Monday morning. The three bids came in at $25,000, $30,000 and $35,000 over the asking price. By letting all the buyers know that others were interested in the property, Margery was able to get a higher price than any comparable apartment had ever sold for in that neighborhood.

The purchase and sale of their homes are normally the biggest negotiations most people ever engage in. Nonetheless, the basic principles of *convince, collaborate,* and *create* still apply. In fact, because of the size and complexity of these transactions, you have even more opportunity to use them to your advantage.

12

Divorce

Don't Get Even, but Get Enough

Jill and her husband, Tom, have been married for 12 years. They have two lovely children, Lauren and David, ages six and eight, whom they both adore. Tom has his own accounting practice. Jill left a public relations job in the city when David was born but recently took a part-time marketing position with a local company. This afternoon Tom called and said he would not be coming home. He wants a divorce. Jill is devastated. In hindsight, she should have seen it coming. Now she does not know what to do.

This scenario, or some variation of it, happens every day in this country. By some estimates, almost 50 percent of all marriages end in divorce. And these days, wives are just as likely to leave their husbands as the reverse. Yet many women who go through divorce, regardless of whether or not they are the initiating party, fare badly. Although the *convince, collaborate,* and *create* principles discussed in this book apply, divorces are different. Divorces are a tragedy for everyone involved. There are no good outcomes—only less-bad ones. Even though your relationship with your spouse, as you have known it, is over, you will have a continuing relationship, particularly if you have children. The nature of that relationship will affect not only your life, but theirs. Therefore, how you negotiate with your spouse matters.

You and your spouse know each other better than anyone else with whom you will ever negotiate. You both know what is important to each other. Moreover, you know each other's "hot buttons," the things that you care about and the things that drive each of you crazy. To complicate matters further, divorces are full of emotion, especially anger. Yet, no matter how emotionally unprepared you are to deal with a divorce, you will have to reach an agreement with your husband, or the courts will impose one on you. That agreement will govern your future dealings, both financial and otherwise, with your husband and your children. You will be forced to make critical decisions at a time when you may not be well equipped to do so. Many women want their lawyer to make these decisions for them. Your lawyer will advise you, but in the end only you can make the key decisions. You can do this well or badly, but you are ultimately responsible for negotiating the divorce settlement. After everything is over, your attorney will get paid and move on to the next case, but you will have to live with the results.

Divorce is all about negotiating. But it is also about relationships: husband-wife, parent-child, lawyer-client, lawyer-lawyer. Moreover, you are not ending the relationship with your spouse. Rather, you are redefining it and negotiating a new relationship. Obviously, if children are involved, there will be a continuing relationship whether you want one or not. Even if you do not have children, you are still defining a financial relationship that may include distribution of property, temporary support, ongoing alimony, and other issues. Often, this financial relationship does not end when the divorce is granted. It can last for many years.

Out of these negotiations two relationships will be forged: the formal legal relationship, the terms of which will be set forth in the divorce decree, and the informal interpersonal relationship between you and your ex-husband that will exist following the divorce. You must pay attention to both. Too often, women sacrifice one or the other. If you do not protect yourself in terms of the formal relationship, you are likely to find yourself regretting the decisions you made. Moreover, you may never recover financially.

On the other hand, if you focus solely on the formally negotiated relationship, you are likely to end up in what Lynn Newsome, a prominent New Jersey divorce lawyer, describes as a "high-conflict post-divorce relationship" in which one of you is always running to court to resolve issues or to try to reopen the financial terms of the settlement. A high conflict post-divorce relationship is the ultimate lose-lose outcome. Both parties remain embroiled in costly legal proceedings and continue their emotional entanglement. Neither party is free to get on with their lives. Moreover, after all the fighting, there may not be enough money left to pay important expenses such as your children's college education.

IF YOU DON'T REACH AGREEMENT, THE COURT WILL DO IT FOR YOU

With that in mind, much can be done to successfully negotiate a divorce settlement. Prepare, use what you know about your spouse, and use time to your advantage. Be empathetic, although not too empathetic, don't be afraid, and avoid acting on your anger. Be creative. Think "outside the box" and hire a lawyer who does the same. In other words, apply the *convince, collaborate,* and *create* principles. However, divorce is a unique situation in which many women either collaborate too much or do not collaborate at all. Either way, they hurt themselves. Therefore, the first task you and your lawyer must accomplish, before you can successfully *collaborate* and *create,* is to *convince* your soon-to-be ex-husband that what you are willing to offer is better than what he would get if he went to trial.

Divorce negotiations are unique in that, if you and your husband cannot reach an agreement, there is a mechanism in place to do so for you. Unlike a situation in which, for example, you and a friend end up taking separate vacations because you can't agree on where to go, if you fail to reach agreement on a divorce settlement, you don't simply go your own ways. The court imposes a settlement on you. When the court imposes a settlement, it is usually worse for both parties than what they would have agreed upon themselves.

Even though the alternative to reaching an agreement yourselves has little to recommend itself, sometimes parties need to actually experience the legal process for themselves before they can actually get down to negotiating. Unfortunately, the contentious nature of the process tends to make it much harder to collaborate when that time comes. The parties must usually first reach a common understanding about the range of possible outcomes that a court might order before being able to use *collaborate* and *create* techniques to craft an agreement that better meets their needs. Your attorney's *convince* skills will play a critical role in making that happen. A good attorney will manage to *convince* without creating additional animosity between you and your spouse.

PREPARE FOR THE REST OF YOUR LIFE

Divorce is a complex process. If you are not the initiating party, you probably have had no occasion to educate yourself about the process or to prepare yourself financially or emotionally to deal with it. Taking the following basic steps will help prepare you to negotiate a settlement that allows you to get on with your life, both financially and emotionally.

Retain a Good Lawyer

This is your first and most crucial priority. But where do you find one? Ask around. Talk with people who have gone through divorces. Ask lawyers you know who specialize in other areas of law. Get a list of lawyers who are active in the matrimonial section of your state bar association. After you have done all this, meet with at least two lawyers. Discuss ahead of time whether that initial consultation will be free, and, if not, what the fee will be.

How will you know a good divorce lawyer when you see one? Start with the qualities that you would want in any attorney: competence, professionalism, and expertise in the particular area of law. Experience in both trying and negotiating divorce cases is important. Good divorce lawyers must know how to try a case but should not be anxious to do so. On the other hand, if they are afraid to take your case to trial, your ability to negotiate a fair settlement will be undermined.

Above all, you must feel comfortable with your attorney. You need to trust his or her judgment. You want someone who understands what is important to you. Look for an attorney who is willing to listen to you, who will be able to deal with you even when you are angry or emotional, and who will tell you when you are being unrealistic. Finally, find a lawyer who is creative and can think "outside the box." Check out prospective lawyers carefully and then trust your instincts.

Part of your preparation is to educate yourself about the process and what you can realistically expect. Your lawyer plays a key role in that education. A good divorce lawyer should able to tell you what different judges will give you, within a reasonable range, in the event that your case goes to trial. To make the trade-offs necessary in any divorce settlement, you need an attorney who can accurately assess what is likely to happen if you go to trial. Be wary of any attorney who paints too optimistic a picture. A good lawyer must be willing to tell you things that you may not want to hear. Any lawyer who does not give you some bad news is probably not being forthright with you.

Keep in mind that it is not your attorney's role to take care of everything for you. Some women, particularly if they have relied on their husbands to take care of financial matters, look to their lawyers to fill that void. Good lawyers are advisers. They cannot make decisions for you. Women who fail to educate themselves about the divorce process and to learn about their finances usually end up being disappointed with their attorney. They find themselves making decisions they are not prepared to make, and, as a result, they often end up regretting those decisions.

Understand Your Family Finances

To work out the financial terms of the divorce, you need financial information. And you want to obtain it as quickly as possible. In most divorces, one party or the other will attempt to understate income and to hide assets. With the extensive records generated today, this becomes harder to do. Nonetheless, it is in your best interest to find out immediately where your family's money comes from and where it goes. This becomes particularly important if your husband owns his own business and is not a W-2 wage earner. Copy all the financial records you can find, including checks, bank statements, credit card statements, and tax returns. Make lists of everything the two of you own, including all your investments. Consider taking steps to safeguard your assets, such as storing your jewelry in a safe deposit box.

Preparation can make the difference between a good settlement and a nasty court battle. Roberta Benjamin, a well-known Massachusetts divorce lawyer and partner in the firm of Benjamin and Benson, described one such case. Her client's husband owned several businesses, including a driving range, which is primarily a cash business. For tax purposes, he claimed that the driving range produced about $250,000 a year in revenues. Her client suspected, based on the way they lived, that it generated much more. When she began to suspect that her husband might be filing for divorce, she had made copies of two year's worth of her husband's daily handwritten notes listing driving range receipts (for example, Sat., May 8, sunny, $2200). This information, in his own handwriting, was crucial in showing that the driving range produced almost $600,000 a year in revenues, not the $250,000 he was claiming. This information enabled Roberta to negotiate a much more favorable settlement for her client.

You must also educate yourself about any financial issues that are likely to arise. Questions about how to divide pensions, 401(k) savings, IRAs, and even stock options are common in divorces today. Some of the decisions that you will be called upon to make require a basic understanding of the tax consequences resulting from those decisions. For example, alimony is taxable, but child support is not. By the same token, your ex-husband will be able to deduct alimony, but not child support. Therefore, whether you label payments as alimony or as child support can have important tax consequences. Dividing up marital property also has tax consequences. Your primary residence may be worth much more than an equally priced vacation home that you rent out, after you take taxes into account. You can sell your marital home for a tax-free profit of up to $500,000 for a married couple or $250,000 if you're single at the time of the sale. However, when you sell the vacation home, you will be taxed on your profit and may have to pay additional taxes if you have depreciated the vacation home for tax purposes. Similarly, $100,000 cash in the bank is worth a lot more than $100,000 in appreciated stocks because you will have to pay capital gains taxes on the profits from the stock when you sell it.

Educate Yourself About the Process

Learn everything you can about the process. Read at least one of the many good books on divorce. Some of these include: *What Every Woman Should Know About Divorce and Custody* (Berkley Publishing, 1998) by Gayle Rosenwald Smith, *Divorce for Dummies* (IDG Books, 1998) by John Ventura and Mary Reed, and *The Smart Divorce* (Golden Books, 1999) by Susan Goldberg and Valerie Colb. Join a support group. Do not be afraid to ask your lawyer questions. However, you can avoid wasting your lawyer's time and your money if you gain a basic understanding of the process first. To achieve a settlement that truly meets your needs, you must be an active participant in the process. And to do that, you must understand it.

Determine What You Would Get If You Were Forced to Go to Trial

The outcome of most divorce cases is predictable within a reasonable range. As mentioned earlier, an experienced divorce lawyer can tell you with a good degree of accuracy what a judge might award in terms of alimony, child support, division of property, and custody. With that information, you can then determine your bottom line. Once you take into account the cost of going to trial, you have a good idea of the minimum settlement that you should be willing to accept. Creativity and collaboration then come into play. Trade-offs can be made. In the end, you should be able to craft an agreement that gives both you and your spouse what is most important to each of you.

Prepare Yourself Emotionally

As part of your preparation, you must recognize that divorce is an emotional time and that you cannot let your emotions drive the negotiations. Most women going through a divorce are either angry or afraid, or both. As a result, their first instinct is to refuse to collaborate on finding mutually acceptable solutions. There is a tendency to want either to strike out or to just capitulate and get it over with. Roberta Benjamin describes this common phenomenon:

> Women, whether housewives or Ph.D.s, come in with economic fears. They see financial ruination, which results in their getting angry. This gets in the way of negotiating. They try to overreach, seeking resolutions that are impossible. Often, if women can feel less victimized, they can get a better settlement.

As much as you might fantasize about vacationing on the Riviera while your ex-husband makes do in a one-room sublet with a hot plate, that is not going to happen. And a father who works 80 hours a week and has missed every school play, little league game, and parent-teacher conference while you stayed at home raising the kids is not going to get sole custody.

Women who do not control their anger and fear tend to prolong the divorce process and make it more contentious. When that happens there is less for everyone. Divorce is not about revenge. It is about getting a deal that allows you to maintain your financial situation and eventually improve it. It also is about agreeing on terms that will govern how your ex-husband deals with you and your children. Your goal should be to agree on terms that you can both live with and that will create as good an environment as possible for your children. If you are angry, you need to get past it. Time, educating yourself about the process, and therapy can help. Consider all of them part of the necessary preparation to negotiate your divorce.

NEGOTIATING YOUR DIVORCE SETTLEMENT

Divorce negotiations are unique in several respects. First, negotiating a settlement can require an extended period of time. Typically, the process takes a minimum of a year and sometimes much longer. Often divorce cases do not get settled until the parties are about to go to trial. What you do while the negotiations are taking place can play a role in how well you fare. Consider the following general advice, but keep in mind that your attorney should advise you about your specific situation.

Negotiate Unemotionally

Even if you have prepared yourself to handle the emotions inherent in the divorce process, there will be moments when you simply can't. Your emotions—be they anger, hurt, despair, impatience, or just plain old fatigue—will overcome you. When that happens, avoid negotiating. Take a break and resume later, or at another time when you are better able to keep things in perspective. Unless you are on the courthouse steps about to go to trial, there will always be another time. A little inconvenience is better than agreeing to something that you will seriously regret later on.

While we were writing this chapter, I was reminded of the one time during our divorce when my ex-wife got emotional—to her detriment. During our marriage, we had accumulated a number of beautiful pieces of furniture at estate sales and antique shows.

We were both particularly fond of one piece, a beautiful Art Deco dining room table that had once been owned by a minor-party presidential candidate. When it came time to negotiate a property settlement, we agreed to take turns choosing the furniture pieces we wanted. We agreed to decide who would get first pick by tossing a coin. So when the day came to split up the furniture, we went to the house with a friend of hers who had agreed to oversee the process and to keep a record of our picks. As luck would have it, I won the coin toss and selected the dining room table. To my surprise, my wife was not just disappointed, she was devastated. At first, she tried to convince me to change my pick. I told her that she should pick and we could revisit the table issue latter. She could not stop focusing on the table. She was beside herself with emotion. She did not care about the rest of her picks and it showed. I had her take a break. I told her friend to talk to her. But even that did not help much. She wanted to be done with it. She ended up unhappy not just about losing the table but about the rest of her picks as well. When she realized how upset she was over losing the table, she should have asked to continue another day when she was in a less emotional state.

Do Not Do Anything Rash

Because divorce is an emotional time, you must proceed cautiously. According to Lynn Newsome, one common mistake that women make is to move out of the house. Unless you have concerns for your safety or the safety of your children, this is seldom a good idea. Leaving the marital home, particularly if you are not the primary breadwinner, dramatically changes your financial situation and puts pressure on you to accept a settlement that might not be in your interest. You must find a place to stay and pay for it. Although your spouse has an incentive to keep paying the mortgage on the marital home, even just to protect his investment in it, he has no reason to pay for your new place. Moreover, the court will take into consideration how much he has to pay to maintain the marital home when determining how much he can contribute to your temporary support. Similarly, leaving the children with your spouse will hurt your chances of being awarded primary custody. When it comes to custody of the children, the party who is taking care of them has a distinct advantage.

If you have been a nonworking wife, consider carefully whether to get a job. Getting a job will reduce your leverage in negotiating the terms of your financial settlement. On the other hand, even if it hurts your legal position, you will probably have no choice but to get a job if you move out of the family home. In most instances, your spouse will not have enough money to pay for 100 percent of your new life, nor will the courts generally require him to do so. You will have to get a job to pay for your new quarters.

Recognize That Emotions, Particularly Guilt and Anger, Can Affect Your Settlement

Feelings of guilt are natural in a divorce, especially if children are involved. Understanding that your spouse may be feeling guilty can help you obtain a favorable settlement. Women tend to feel uncomfortable taking advantage of someone else's feelings of guilt, whereas men have little problem using any edge they might have in a negotiation. In divorce cases, however, many women are angry and only too happy to use their ex-husband's feelings of guilt to get what they want. Unfortunately, their anger often prevents them from doing so effectively.

Many men who leave their wives are involved with, or have been involved with, another woman. Often the man is not particularly proud of this. Moreover, when children are involved, a man almost always feels some guilt, regardless of his feelings toward his spouse. Men also tend to get over feelings easily, so if you display anger and bitterness toward him, he will quickly stop feeling guilty. That type of behavior makes it easy for him to justify his actions by blaming you for causing the divorce.

Sometimes you can exploit your husband's guilt feelings by pushing through a settlement quickly before they dissipate. At other times, you can take advantage of this emotion by simply doing nothing. For example, if your husband moves out of the house but continues to pay the bills and deposits money into the joint account as always, it may be in your interest to maintain the status quo because he may be giving you more temporary support than a court would order. Moreover, if the situation continues for any length of time, you will have a basis for seeking an equivalent amount of permanent support. One attorney we know advises her clients to simply "ride the gravy train until it stops."

One obvious caveat: If you are the spouse having the affair or if you are the one who is initiating the divorce, you will not be able to call upon your spouse's feelings of guilt. He is more likely to be feeling anger. However, in those instances, he may well try to use your feelings of guilt to get you to accept less than a fair settlement, so be on your guard.

Timing Is Everything in Life and in Divorce

Time is another element that you can use effectively in negotiating your divorce. If your spouse is the one who has filed for divorce, he may be in a greater hurry than you are to conclude the proceedings. If he has moved out of the house, maintaining two homes may be causing financial strain. Or, it could just be that, as the party initiating the divorce, he is more anxious to get on with his life. Your awareness that time can play a role in his willingness to reach an agreement provides you with a distinct advantage.

Certain negotiations get resolved only when one or both the parties has had enough. To the extent that your spouse is in a hurry, use time to your advantage. If he is not, you may have to wait until he is ready. But if you find yourself feeling that you have had enough and just want out, do not give in to that emotion.

Knowledge Is Power, So Use It Wisely

As we mentioned above, divorce negotiations are unique because the parties know each other so well. As they say in the superhero comics, "This power can be used for good or for evil." Unfortunately, when we are in the throes of divorce, we tend to use this knowledge to push each other's buttons. Women may be tempted to use the children to get to their husbands. Men may try to threaten or bully their spouse into submission. Such tactics seldom have the intended effect.

Sometimes women try to deny their former spouses visitation rights, or they refuse to tell them about the children's activities. Using your children as leverage in a divorce, or, worse yet, to get even with your former spouse, does not work and only makes resolving the divorce more difficult. Courts see right through it. When one party tries to use children to gain advantage, it does nothing except hurt the children. Always bear in mind that, even if your ex-husband is the worst person on the face of the earth, he is still the father of your children. Negotiate accordingly.

Conversely, men often try to intimidate their wives by threatening a custody battle. However, unless there are unusual circumstances, your lawyer should be able to quickly reassure you that your ex-husband has almost no chance of getting sole custody of your children. Those threats are meaningless in court and are usually counterproductive in the negotiating process.

Recently, we were talking with a divorced friend who is a very successful consultant. We asked whether her former husband, a successful doctor, had tried to intimidate her during the divorce. She said he had threatened to "ruin" her. He warned her that, by the time he was finished, she would never recover financially. That made her angry, and his threats had the opposite effect of what he intended; they just made her want to fight back. She added, however, that now, years later, he had begun acting much nicer. While he owed her several thousand dollars in back alimony, he was being so nice she felt uncomfortable pressing him to pay her. This is one way in which men can use their relationship with you to your detriment, if you let them. Typically, it is not your husband's threats that should worry you. Rather, the time to keep up your guard is when he is treating you well.

First Convince, Then Collaborate

Once you get beyond the emotions involved, divorce is ideally suited to collaborative solutions. At one time, at least, you were probably in love with your husband, and he was in love with you. If you have children, you will have to see and deal with each other for years to come. You both have a variety of interests to resolve. Collaboration offers numerous opportunities for you to satisfy one another's needs without sacrificing your own.

Finding ways to reduce your taxes can provide more money to each of you; your attorney can advise you about these opportunities. Roberta Benjamin offers an example of how this can work. She was representing a woman whose husband was earning a large salary at the time of the divorce. He had agreed to pay a significant amount of child support, but then he lost his job and eventually had to take a much lower-paying position. He filed a motion to reduce his child support payments. It was clear that the court would have to grant that motion in some form. Instead, the parties simply agreed to recast the child support as tax-deductible alimony. The husband saved enough in taxes that he did not have to reduce the total amount he was paying. And because the wife was in a much lower tax bracket, the change had only a slight impact on her.

By thinking about your husband's interests in a collaborative way, you can also often find ways in the course of your daily interactions to satisfy your needs as well as his. Sometimes all you need do is ask in the right way. If, for example, your son's soccer team is going out of town to play in a Thanksgiving tournament and you would find it difficult to pay for his bus and hotel room, you might ask your ex-husband if he would like to take your son to the tournament. You may be surprised at how willing he might be to do that.

What are the keys to reaching a collaborative settlement? First, determine what you want and what you can reasonably expect to get. As mentioned above, your lawyer should be able to tell you what you can realistically expect to get if you go to trial. Once you know that, you can begin the process of finding out what is important to your husband. The fact that you know him so well is a tremendous advantage at this point. Then you can begin the process of maximizing your respective interests. Keep in mind that collaborating does not mean giving up things that are important to your future, and to which you are entitled, for the sake of maintaining some form of friendly relationship with your ex-husband. Rather, your goal is to reach a fair settlement that maximizes both of your respective interests to the greatest extent possible.

WHEN YOU CANNOT ACHIEVE YOUR OBJECTIVES BY COLLABORATING, CREATE

Because of the emotional nature of divorce and the inherent contentiousness of the legal process, creativity can play a critical role in reaching an agreement. As in any negotiation, coming up with an alternative proposal, or even just describing what you are asking for in another way, can get the other side to accept something that was previously unacceptable. When my ex-wife and I were finalizing our divorce settlement, I refused to pay any additional alimony or child support. Even though I was adamant about not increasing the financial settlement that had been proposed, her lawyer was effectively able to tap into my sense of guilt by saying, "Look, when your 10-year-old daughter comes to you and says she wants to go to soccer camp but her mom says she can't afford it, are you really going to tell her she can't go? Since you're going to pay anyway, to settle this, let's just agree you will pay up to X dollars a year to send your daughter to camp for the next three years." When she put it that way, I not only agreed—I also harbored no resentment about paying that money so that my daughter could go to camp.

Creativity can come into play in many ways. Lynn Newsome described a case in which the husband and wife could not agree on anything. The husband was insisting on joint custody and would accept nothing less. He was adamant on that point. Lynn was representing the wife, who had been responsible for making all the decisions involving the children during the marriage. The wife was afraid that her husband would use his joint custody rights to harass her. Based on his behavior during the settlement negotiations, she had legitimate reason for concern. Lynn was able to resolve that issue by the creative use of language. She proposed that the parties have "joint custody" but that the mother, her client, have "sole decision-making authority" for most aspects of the children's lives. This satisfied the husband and avoided a custody battle.

Much of this chapter has focused on women who are not the primary breadwinner, which is probably more common than the opposite situation. However, it is becoming more and more common for women to make more money than their spouses. Do these same negotiating approaches work for them? The answer is yes, with a twist. You can use all the prejudices built into the system to protect nonworking women to your advantage. For example, a normal, healthy man who is the primary caregiver for your children will be assumed to be capable of going to work and earning a decent living. Most judges will have much less sympathy for, and be much less generous with, a nonworking man than they would with a similarly situated woman.

Plan for Your Future

Creativity requires looking at the big picture and taking the long-term view. Some women, often to their detriment, adopt a short-term focus when they are going through a divorce. They're just trying to get through the next few years, take care of the kids, and get them through college. Others look only at the short term because they assume they will remarry. Consider where you will be 10 or 20 years from now. You want to be able to maintain your present lifestyle or, at least, something that approaches it. Realistically, you and your husband will both probably end up reducing your lifestyle at first, but he will eventually improve his. You need to negotiate so that you will as well.

Women who have not worked outside the home sometimes fear going into the workplace. Many programs and other support are available to help women make this transition. Although your lawyer may advise you that it is not in your interest to begin one of these programs before the terms of your divorce are finalized, you should educate yourself about what is available.

Most men are more than willing to agree to pay for their wife's education or job training because they assume these will reduce their overall financial obligations. In most cases, an agreement that your husband will pay for additional education and job training will have little impact on the settlement. But it may have a significant impact on your ability to build a successful future.

For purposes of determining alimony, most attorneys ask judges to assume that a nonworking homemaker is capable of earning a certain amount of income even if she has never worked outside the home, at least if she is under 45. Because working mothers are now the norm and people are working much longer, this trend is likely to continue. So you might as well take advantage of education and training opportunities that will help you build a better life—and have your spouse pay for it. A good time to raise that issue is when your husband's lawyer asks that your ability to get a job be taken into consideration in determining alimony, as he or she probably will.

It is important to get what you need, not just to survive but to prosper. That means knowing what you are entitled to and thinking expansively and creatively to ensure your future.

13

Empower Yourself

A Three-Step Program
for Better Negotiating

As you are learning to become a better negotiator, you will go through three stages: illumination, progression, and transformation. In the illumination stage, you learn the skills you need. In the progression stage, you practice those skills until you master them. In the transformation stage, negotiating becomes second nature, like driving—whenever there is a need, you automatically call on those skills. In this final chapter, we set forth a simple, three-step program to help you transform yourself into an effective negotiator.

The end of the chapter offers a checklist to help you to measure your progress. Familiarize yourself with each of the skills and attitudes set forth on the checklist. Pay special attention to nurturing the proper negotiating attitudes. Measure your progress periodically by rating yourself on each of the listed skills and attitudes. Then focus on those that require work. In no time, you will find yourself becoming a better negotiator. You need not have mastered every specific negotiating skill to negotiate well. With the right attitude, you will be able to use the skills you have mastered to achieve your objectives while you add additional ones to your repertory. As you master each additional skill, you will find yourself becoming more effective as a negotiator.

ILLUMINATION

As you begin to learn about negotiating, the process of illumination may automatically result in change. In some situations, just knowing what to do is enough. Learning new skills will often allow you to do things that you never realized you could do. Moreover, simply becoming aware of what we are doing wrong sometimes enables us to correct the problem or break bad habits. Like shining a light on something you have never seen before, once you have been made aware of what you have been doing, you can never go back to doing things the same old way. You can gain illumination through reading, studying, and watching others negotiate.

Study

Negotiating is a skill, and, like any skill, it can be learned. Reading this book is your first step toward becoming an effective negotiator. Studying the material we have presented here will enable you to negotiate successfully with anyone. The tools to handle any negotiating situation are right here for you to use. However, if you are having difficulty understanding certain aspects of the negotiating process, or you just want to further your education, we recommend the following books:

Getting to Yes: Negotiating Agreement Without Giving In (2nd ed., Penguin Books, 1991) by Fisher, Ury, and Patton, is the bible of win-win negotiating, and anyone who wants to master the art of collaborative negotiating should study this book.

Another book we like, and I'm glad we both agree because I would recommend it anyway, is my previous book, *Get More Money On Your Next Job: 25 Proven Strategies for Getting More Money, Better Benefits, and Greater Job Security* (McGraw-Hill, 1997). Besides helping you to increase your earning power, it also illustrates many of the general principles of effective negotiating with examples drawn from the employment context.

If you're navigating your way through the corporate jungle, you can have no better guide than Gail Evans. In *Play Like a Man, Win Like a Woman* (Broadway Books, 2000), she advises women about what will and will not work for them if they want to succeed in the business world. Although she does not focus specifically on how to negotiate, her insights will help you when you negotiate with your boss, with your coworkers, with your subordinates, with your customers, with your suppliers, and with other business people you meet along the way.

Finally, we recommend John Gray's *Men Are from Mars, Women Are from Venus: A Practical Guide for Improving Communication and Getting What You Want in Your Relationships* (HarperCollins, 1992). If you want to master the art of negotiating in a relationship, this book is a must for your personal library. Negotiating in relationships differs from other types of negotiations in part because of the emotions involved. His insights into the ways that men and women can communicate and relate better by recognizing their differences are extremely useful.

Observe

Find good, skilled negotiators—at work, among your friends, and in charitable and civic organizations, as well as among those with whom you interact on a daily basis—and watch them negotiate. Observe them. Spend time with them. If you can, arrange

to work with them on projects. Pay attention to how they interact with people. Watch what they say and do. You'll be amazed
at how much you can learn just by watching good negotiators.

> When I was growing up, I always tried to listen when my
> father was negotiating. Afterwards, I would ask lots of questions
> to try to understand what was going on—what he was trying to
> achieve, and why he said and did certain things. These experi-
> ences helped me to learn which approaches work with different
> types of people and which ones do not. I still draw on those early
> lessons today.

Many of the women we interviewed did the same thing.
Cincinnati Bengals executive Katie Blackburn describes a similar
experience. When she was in high school, she would sit in when
her dad was negotiating with players' agents. She would run figures for him and listen to him talk to the agents. She says that,
even today, when an agent says something during negotiations,
in her mind she hears her father's response to a similar question.
It helps her know what to say.

We also learn by watching the people with whom we work.
When I started out as a young attorney in a law firm, I was given
the opportunity to work with the head of the firm's litigation
department. He had an unassuming personality and a quiet style,
very different from my own. Yet he was an exceptional negotiator.
He had a way of gaining people's trust and getting them to
believe him. I had many chances to observe him when he negotiated. Many of the things I do today when I negotiate, I learned
from watching him.

Whenever we negotiate with seasoned negotiators, we not only
pay attention to the substance of what is being discussed, but also
observe what they do. We learn lessons from what does and does
not work for us, but also from watching what the other side does

as well. Consider every negotiation a success if you learn from it. If you study and watch, you will find illumination.

PROGRESSION

To master particular skills or develop the right attitude for negotiating, illumination is not enough. You cannot master negotiating skills such as active listening, purposeful questioning, or identifying interests unless you practice them. Knowing when and how to use such skills as anchoring, granting concessions, reflecting back, and coupling interests takes time and effort. It does not occur overnight. To become proficient with these skills, you must use them.

The mental attitudes that support effective negotiating are even harder to change. You can develop them only through practice. You must *experience* the success that comes from being confident, or at least acting that way. You have to *feel* the power that comes from demonstrating your willingness to walk away. Only then will those attitudes become a part of who you are and how you negotiate. You can learn how to prepare for various types of negotiations by reading this book. That is illumination. But only through experience will you be able to go into a negotiation confident in the belief that you are prepared for whatever the other side might throw at you. That attitude can only be achieved through experience. Learning to ask, to negotiate for yourself, to say no, and to take calculated risks requires practice. The more you work at inculcating those attitudes in yourself, the more comfortable you will become with them. Soon you will wonder why you ever had difficulty doing those things.

To facilitate your progression, we recommend that you take a negotiating course or seminar. Many colleges and business schools offer such courses. In my negotiating seminars, I build in simulations and exercises designed to provide students with opportunities to practice negotiating in a variety of different set-tings. Most negotiating programs include these types of exercises.

When it comes to learning to negotiate, there is nothing like learning by doing. Participating in negotiating simulations and receiving feedback are excellent ways to develop the skills and attitudes necessary to succeed as a negotiator. Role-playing in a controlled environment offers opportunities to try different things, to experiment with different approaches, and to observe how your fellow students handle similar situations. So if you have a chance to enroll in a negotiating seminar, take advantage of it.

Similarly, if you need to improve your persuasive skills, pub-lic speaking courses in which students are required to give pre-sentations can be helpful. These will increase your confidence as well as improving your delivery. Or consider joining a group like Toastmasters in which you practice giving speeches to other members.

Seek out every opportunity to practice negotiating. Go out of your way to find low-risk negotiating opportunities—situations in which even a poor performance will have no serious conse-quences. See what you can negotiate. Start with little things. Be conscious of what you are doing. Experiment. Observe your feel-ings. Try different approaches. See what works for you. Focus on the skills and attitudes that require more practice. Negotiate with your husband or boyfriend. See if you can get him to take you to the ballet or to that Japanese restaurant you want to try. Go to a flea market and practice anchoring and walking away. See if you can get the store manager to reduce the price of the table you are looking at because it has a scratch. Negotiate with street vendors.

Treat every situation as a chance to learn and practice. The worst that can happen is someone will say no. In that case, you are no worse off than you were before. You will be surprised, however, by how often you get what you ask for. More important, you will become not only a better, more skilled negotiator, but also a more comfortable and confident one as well.

After you negotiate, review how well you did. Identify which skills you used and evaluate your success with them. Which were most effective? Which did not work the way you thought they would? What could you have done differently? Examine your mistakes. Look at whether you were able to manifest the proper attitudes. Refer to the checklist at the end of this chapter to measure your progress. Focus first on improving the skills and attitudes that come most easily, then move on to those that are more difficult. Pick one skill or attitude each week and work on it. Before long you will see a significant improvement in your negotiating. And, with practice, you will move through progression to transformation.

TRANSFORMATION

If you complete the processes of illumination and progression, you will have gone a long way toward integrating the habits and attitudes of a successful negotiator into your nature. However, what should you do if you try but you just cannot seem to "get it?"

With skills you can usually gain mastery through additional study or practice. You may require extra work—such as taking another class or rereading sections of this book. One-on-one training may be the answer. As a teacher, I find that videotaping students while they are negotiating can be a dramatic help. Watching themselves negotiate and having someone critique them often provide the insights needed to master skills that are eluding them.

Changing attitudes is more difficult. Being able to say no is a good example. At first, it may be difficult for you to learn to say no. Through the illumination process, though, you will come to understand the importance of saying no if your interests have not been met. Initially, you have to force yourself to do it. After a while, it gets easier. In fact, most women quickly find it liberating to be able to say no. Some people, though, just cannot manage it. They know they should, but they cannot bring themselves to do it. They may have a particularly difficult time saying no to people with whom they have a relationship. So they give in when they should say no and feel angry and resentful as a result. This is just one example of how we sometimes continue doing things that we know are not working for us because we cannot seem to stop. We have learned the skills, and we know what we should be doing, but we just cannot seem to develop the attitudes needed to succeed.

Changing those attitudes requires believing in yourself. Without that belief, you cannot be a successful negotiator. All the other requisite attitudes depend on that. If you believe in yourself, you will believe that saying no is the right thing to do and you will have the confidence to say it.

If challenged, women often have difficulty sustaining their belief that what they are doing is right. This is particularly difficult when they are faced with repeated and aggressive challenges to the fairness of their position, or when they must repeatedly say no to a proposal being pushed by the other side. Men know this and use it to their advantage. When that occurs, consider seeking another person's opinion to reassure yourself that you are being fair. Ultimately, to be successful, you must develop sufficient confidence to avoid doubting yourself when you are challenged. Until you build up your self-confidence sufficiently so that you no longer question your instincts, work on developing an inner voice to reassure you. Say the same things to yourself that a friend would say. Eventually you will undergo a transformation, and you will internalize that inner voice. Most of the time, your first instincts are correct. Using this technique will help build the confidence you need to be an effective negotiator.

➤─┼─◆─┼─○─┼─◆─┼─◄

In her 1997 commencement address at Wellesley, Oprah Winfrey advised the graduating seniors: "You become what you believe." To succeed not only as a negotiator but as a person, you have to believe in yourself.

As a young woman, I tend to look more to Oprah Winfrey than to Wayne Gretzky as a role model. But both share an understanding of the importance of believing in yourself—of not being afraid to try and of not being afraid to fail. That is what negotiating is all about. Whenever I get nervous about asking for something, I still hear my father's words when I was growing up: "What's the worst thing that could happen?" The worst is usually no worse than where I would be if I did not try. Asking yourself that question should help you overcome some of your fears. No one likes being told no, and no one likes failing, but the only real failure in life is letting fear keep you from going after what you want.

➤─┼─◆─┼─○─┼─◆─┼─◄

Anna Lloyd, President and Executive Director of the Committee of 200, has an all female staff, most of whom are fairly young. When they have to negotiate, she helps them to believe in themselves by sitting and talking it through with them. Then she has them go home and commit their strategy to paper by writing out what they want to accomplish and how they propose to get there. If you do not have someone like Anna to help when you are preparing, follow psychologist Patricia Farrell's advice and use "self-talk." Convince yourself that your position is right and that you can get what you are seeking. If you can convince yourself, it will be easy to convince others.

Among the other attitude-changing techniques that you can try are books and tapes to help you build the confidence and self-esteem necessary to change your attitudes. Some useful books are *The Confidence Factor* (Mile High Press, 2001) by Judith Briles and John Malin, *The Six Pillars of Self Esteem* (Doubleday Dell, 1995) by Nathan Branden, and *The Four Agreements* (Amber-Allen Pub., 1997) by Don Miguel Ruiz. Workshops that focus on those areas are also available. Tony Robbins's Personal Power program is just one of many that may help you to develop the positive attitudes you need when you negotiate.

Personal coaches can help you to change your attitude. They can "hold your feet to the fire" and help you break through previously self-imposed limits. Coaches knowledgeable in the art of negotiating can help you develop your negotiating skills as well. You may also want to take up an activity such as acting, dancing, or yoga that will enhance your confidence and self-esteem.

Finally, if you remain stuck with self-defeating negotiating attitudes and behavior such as the fear of asking for what you want or the inability to say no, you may require personal transformation in other areas of your life. Support groups can help you understand and change deep-seated behavior patterns arising from early negative messages held deep in your subconscious. Therapy can also promote transformation. You can locate an appropriate therapist through a doctor's referral, or through a church, synagogue, or community center. Both one-on-one therapy and weekend workshops or ongoing seminars can be life-changing. Community colleges may also offer courses in personal change.

Success as a negotiator is part skill and part attitude. We have given you the skills to negotiate well. We have outlined the attitudes you need and how you can go about developing them. We have set forth a program that you can use to illuminate, progress, and transform yourself into an effective negotiator. If you are positive and believe in yourself, there is little that you cannot accomplish. This is just as true in negotiating as it is in life. If you follow the advice in this book, study negotiating, watch people negotiate, practice and develop the right attitudes, you will become the type of negotiator you want to be—at work, at home, with your boss, with your husband, with your children, and with everyone else in your life. Becoming a better negotiator will improve your total quality of life—your relationships, your income, your free time, your parenting—every aspect of your life.

Appendix

Negotiating Skills and Attitudes Checklist

Rated on a scale of 1—10	Illumination (Understand 1—4)	Progression (Practicing 5—7)	Transformation (Mastery 8—10)
GENERAL ATTITUDES			
Confidence	_____	_____	_____
Preparation	_____	_____	_____
Willingness to Walk Away	_____	_____	_____
SPECIFIC ATTITUDES			
Able to Be Myself	_____	_____	_____
Not Afraid to Ask	_____	_____	_____
Able to Negotiate for Myself	_____	_____	_____
Maintains Focus on Goals	_____	_____	_____
Avoids Empathy Trap	_____	_____	_____
Able to Say No	_____	_____	_____
Emotions Do Not Interfere	_____	_____	_____

Takes Reasonable Risks	_____	_____	_____
Uses Humor	_____	_____	_____
Take People as I Find Them	_____	_____	_____

CONVINCE

ACTIVE LISTENING SKILLS

Listening Under	_____	_____	_____
Reflecting back	_____	_____	_____
Clarifying	_____	_____	_____
Encouraging	_____	_____	_____
Acknowledging Effort	_____	_____	_____
Recognizing Feelings	_____	_____	_____
Summarizing	_____	_____	_____

PURPOSEFUL QUESTIONING SKILLS

Open-ended Questions	_____	_____	_____
Using Silence	_____	_____	_____
Columbo Technique	_____	_____	_____
Repetition in Question Form	_____	_____	_____
Answering with a Question	_____	_____	_____
Using Questions to Persuade	_____	_____	_____

ANCHORING SKILLS

Determining Range	_____	_____	_____
Anchoring Initial Offer	_____	_____	_____

RHETORICAL SKILLS

Developing Themes	_____	_____	_____
Highlighting Benefits	_____	_____	_____

Tailoring Arguments	_____	_____	_____
Leading to Conclusion	_____	_____	_____
Anticipating Objections	_____	_____	_____
Using Experts	_____	_____	_____
Adjusting the Message	_____	_____	_____
Managing Expectations	_____	_____	_____
Using Concessions	_____	_____	_____

COLLABORATE

COLLABORATIVE SKILLS

Developing Relationships	_____	_____	_____
Leveraging Other Relationships	_____	_____	_____
Determining Interests	_____	_____	_____
Using Value Differences	_____	_____	_____
Trading	_____	_____	_____
Expanding the Pie	_____	_____	_____
Coupling Interests	_____	_____	_____
Identifying New Options	_____	_____	_____

CREATE

CREATIVE SKILLS

Examining Assumptions	_____	_____	_____
Exploring Other Alternatives	_____	_____	_____
Trying Different Things	_____	_____	_____
Creating New Paradigms	_____	_____	_____

Index

About the Authors

Lee Miller, a graduate of Harvard Law School, is the Managing Director of the Advanced Human Resources Groups, Inc., where he provides training in the art of negotiating and works with companies and individuals in developing and implementing negotiating strategies. He also teaches negotiating classes in the MBA program at Seton Hall University and is the former Chair of the International Association of Corporate and Professional Recruiters and the Committee on Employment Law of the American Corporate Counsel Association, New York Chapter. Mr. Miller can be contacted at ahrgrp@earthlink.net.

Jessica Miller is an investment banker with Deutsche Bank Securities. A magna cum laude graduate of Virginia Tech, with a degree in Business Administration, she is an outstanding negotiator in her own right. She is also Lee's eldest daughter.